# AMBLESIDE
# THE GRUFF GUIDE

– to a unique community in the
Lake District – for the curious
and discerning

by Paul Renouf

Illustrations by

Sarah Waterhouse

To Richard

Paul Renouf

Published by Ambleside Online
Bracklyn, Millans Park, Ambleside, LA22 9AG, UK
www.amblesideonline.co.uk

Text content copyright Paul Renouf
Illustrations copyright Sarah Waterhouse
www.waterarthouse.co.uk
With contributions by Dr. Paul Davies
of Ambleside Health Centre

First printed 2017 by Badger Press Ltd
Longlands Rd, Bowness-on-Windermere, LA23 3AS, UK

ISBN 978-0-9957257-0-6

Cover illustration: Untitled (Bridge House, Ambleside)
by Kurt Schwitters
(courtesy of Armitt Library and Museum, Ambleside)

* not that public

# Foreword

It has been said that guidebooks, rather than pointing us towards new experiences can in fact put us at one step removed from them. Yet, since Thomas Gray's 'Journal of his Tour in the Lake District' in 1775, guidebooks have rained down upon the area, from the personal and idiosyncratic to the detailed and comprehensive. The earliest were guides for the 'picturesque' tourist, satirized while still warm from the press. Wordsworth wrote his in 1807 for 'persons of taste and feeling for landscape'. Short on detailed tourist information, he happily directed his readers to other contemporary guidebook writers such as William Green to deal with this 'humble and tedious' task. In contrast, Harriet Martineau in her 1855 Guide showed more interest in the availability of hot baths in the hotels than the aesthetics of landscape, and characterised the native population as primitive, ignorant and drink sodden. Modern guidebooks despite their infinite variety often seem a little anodyne by comparison. This Gruff Guide is an alternative to the generality.

It is written by an insider, for anyone, resident or visitor, with a sense of curiosity about Ambleside, a desire to peep behind the curtains and explore its hidden nooks and crannies. It reminds us that although undoubtedly struggling under the weight of Gore-Tex and second 'homes', this is still a community, and like all communities slightly baffling to the outsider. It has its own dynamics, its ancient feuds and modern anxieties. This guide also, through its liberal use of the excellent Ambleside Oral History Archive, goes a step further than most, it allows its subject to do something rare – speak for itself.

Deborah Walsh,
Curator – The Armitt Museum and Library, Ambleside

# Introduction

Here is firsthand, up to date and relevant info from **local people who know**, and not just about accommodation and eating out. We take you beyond the mundane listings of hotels, B&Bs and attractions into the hidden psyche of this fascinating community with its dark secrets and repressed passions. We describe little known places and discuss famous residents from the past. We quote first hand memories of local people born as far back as 1880 describing events, their jobs and their daily lives. We also bring you up to date, outlining some of the issues which affect us today.

So if you like Ambleside, or even love it as some people say they do, you cannot afford to be without this book and the treasures it contains. And if you dislike Ambleside, we hope your opinion may be altered hereby, but one thing is certain – if it isn't, we won't be very concerned because we know you can't please everyone.

# Contents

Scotland

Northumberland

Cumbria

Durham

Yorkshire

Lancashire

Cheshire

Derbyshire

Nottinghamshire

Lincolnshire

Shropshire

Staffordshire

Leicestershire

Norfolk

Worcestershire

Warwickshire

Northamptonshire

Cambridgeshire

Suffolk

Hereford shire

Bedfordshire

Hertfordshire

Essex

Gloucestershire

Buckinghamshire

Oxfordshire

London

Avon

Wiltshire

Berkshire

Surrey

Kent

Wales

Somerset

Hampshire

Sussex

Devon

Dorset

Cornwall

# Where is Ambleside?

SCOTLAND

CARLISLE

NORTHUMBERLAND

Carlisle

Maryport

Wigton

EDEN

DURHAM

Workington

ALLERDALE

Penrith

Whitehaven

Keswick

Brough

COPELAND

Ambleside

Seascale

Windermere

NORTH YORKSHIRE

SOUTH LAKELAND

Barrow in Furness

Kirkby Lonsdale

3

# CHAPTER I

# Where and what is Ambleside?

So where is Ambleside?... it is situated in the north west of England in the county of Cumbria. It is also right in the centre of the country's most beautiful National Park, the Lake District. Only five hours drive or four hours rail from London, less than two from Manchester or Liverpool, one hour from the Scottish border, three from Edinburgh...avoid the rest of England (too crowded) and speed instead to unique, relaxing Ambleside, where you will find fine food, wine and ale to complement the glorious lakeside mountain setting of this historic... er... sorry, prehistoric community. It was here before the Roman occupation, which lasted 400 years, it was devastated but survived and prospered under the Viking invasion and it will be here after the tourist invasion, which so far has lasted only 200 years. (Blame Wordsworth for this latter invasion please, not the Tourism officials. As the French revolution and Napoleonic wars cut off the

English gentry from their European Grand Tour, their writers, poets and artists began to extol the glory of Lakeland, creating as they did so the necessary myths which are their stock in trade and which survive to this day to persuade the discerning visitor of the rare quality of this landscape.)

'ROUND AMBLESIDE YOU WILL INDEED FIND HILLS AND WATERFALLS ... BRASS BANDS PLAY UNDER YOUR HOTEL WINDOW, CHAR-A-BANC WAGONETTES AND BREAKS OF ALL COLOURS RATTLE ABOUT WITH TOURISTS' — DICKENS

Holding out stubbornly against this endless horde of apparently tireless walkers, climbers and futile seekers after the long-gone romance of the English countryside, the ageing locals (peasantry, as the 19th century writers would insist) gallantly strive to ignore the alien cultures which mass tourism imposes on their quiet lives, complaining only, as they reap the doubtful material rewards, that "t' spot's thrang wi' t' boogers" (Eng. "there are rather too many of them, don't you think?"). Regretfully, the numbers of these fine local characters dwindle year by year as they join their old friends in the graveyard, to be replaced by the only people who can afford to live here now. And you know who you are.

# CHAPTER 2

# Visitor information – eating, shopping and mucking about

**Public warning!** The people of Ambleside welcome visitors – we need your money and we often get to know and like some of you! So far be it from us to wish to insult our visitors but we do want to make the point that we are a community, not a resort. As such, we prefer to have our customs and peculiarities respected and our territory treated with consideration. Although we are in England's greatest National Park, every acre is owned by somebody and much of it is private property which you are not supposed to enter uninvited.

**And a warm public welcome!** As a tourist centre Ambleside has a long and favourable history. For well over 150 years the town earned a living catering for visitors, giving them mostly what they wanted, provided they didn't mind what they got. The last thirty five years have seen a revolution in tourist provision however, as upgrading of catering and accommodation at all levels has been led by the market and by encouragement from official bodies. Few could nowadays claim that they cannot enjoy the level of catering they expect, if they don't mind paying for it. All sectors of the market, from campers to gourmets, will find satisfactory establishments in Ambleside and its outlying hamlets and villages. Just don't expect five star facilities in simple guest houses!

In addition to all its attractions, Ambleside is also a very convenient starting point for excursions, walking, cycling or driving, into all areas of the Lake District, situated as it is at the hub of the area's road system.

The town is easily reached by road, being 20 miles from the M6 motorway, and is served by several bus services, including National Express. Rail travel is to Windermere, four miles away with easy bus and taxi access. There is a Manchester Airport/Windermere rail link, change at Oxenholme.

If it hadn't been for Wordsworth and his antipathy to opening up the Lake District to the hoi polloi the trains would have continued to Ambleside and possibly even to

Grasmere. What a boon that would be today when car usage is being (unsuccessfully) discouraged.

KEEPING THE HOI POLLOI AT BAY

# Where to Stay, Eat and Drink

The proliferation of guides, maps and books on the Lake District was the main reason for having to rebuild the British Library, allegedly. There is a frighteningly long list of all types, from pretty picture books to walking guides to accommodation to literary to art. Lakeland is a publishers' paradise – sell 2000 hardbacks in 12 months for a quick buck then remainder the rest.

The web has gone down the book publishers' road, spawning a proliferation of sites all claiming to be the best, most authoritative, official guide to the Lake District. But none beat Ambleside Online if it's Ambleside you want to know about! It is without doubt the most comprehensive, informative and entertaining community website in cyberspace.

Ambleside Online website uniquely lists every business in the Ambleside area, including all accommodation and catering establishments. To find bed and board, go to their Accommodation pages, where all businesses are listed, many with display ads, web links and direct booking/enquiry facilities.

Until the turn of the 21st century Ambleside's entrepreneurs were mainly independent traders. Since then a number of franchises have moved in to exploit the coffee shop phenomenon — at weekends we witness visitors wandering around holding take-away lattes and Americanos as they window shop, a strange sight — it's as if nowadays we are incomplete without being seen to consume something. Among the most successful independent entrepreneurs is Mr Derek Hook. His stylish enterprises, including Zeffirelli's five cinema screens, his restaurants, and latterly his guest house Ambleside Manor, have surely done more to popularise Ambleside as a visitor destination than any amount of public money poured into official promotions. And yet this modest man seeks no limelight, no recognition, no power or influence. Above Zeff's restaurant the Jazz Bar weekly features live folk, rock, but mainly jazz bands, including some world class acts, usually free of charge (though you are supposed to buy drink and possibly food).

# What to do

This is a subject of some complexity. It depends on what you are. Some locals often wonder why anyone bothers to come, but they have long since taken their surroundings for granted.

Mainstream activities in the Lake District have an outdoor emphasis, combined with quiet enjoyment of the magnificent scenery and its literary and artistic heritage. The area is justly famous as an escape for stressed out urban dwellers, who come to enjoy a little solitude as they walk the hills. Or some of them do – others come in great groups and talk incessantly as they walk. Specialist shops, particularly in Ambleside, offer a welcome variation on High Street chains, while galleries and small museums allow quiet contemplation. The area is equally famous for its high quality mountaineering opportunities, Ambleside being the gateway to the famous Langdale valley, a major rock climbing centre and one of the country's most popular upland walking areas.

A good stay in Ambleside for the general visitor might include something of all these interests, combined with an occasional dinner in one of many high quality restaurants and a sampling of the vast selection of real ales available in the pubs. If you are a sober, contemplative, quiet sort of person who enjoys fine landscape, natural beauty and healthy exercise, you couldn't come to better place. If you are a bon viveur, you will not be disappointed in the standards and wide range of catering and accommodation available here. If you are a crag rat, you won't need telling about the great climbs of every grade. If you just want a good time, relaxed atmosphere and a disco at night, we've got all that too.

If the great outdoors is what you want, at local shops and info centres you can buy books and leaflets telling you how to get on to the fells (northern English hills/mountains). For a taste of Lakeland walking, have a look at our walks pages. Mostly you don't need leaflets, you just put one foot before the other in a forwards and upwards direction until the only next step is down. Then you will gaze in wonder at the spectacle below you and vow never to do it again – unless, that is, you become hooked.

At this point you will become a danger to the local community, because before long you will be so addicted to walking hills, even climbing crags, that you will want to buy a second home here and do some ill-paid local out of the chance of a first one. You may then eventually join a local environmental pressure group and complain when the District Council wants to build new starter homes for locals. Believe it, people do!

If you lack the confidence to hill walk, you can pay to go on guided walks. There are at least 3 local organisations happy to take your money for showing you how to do this. Do a web search if you want this service.

There is nothing made that you can't get here in the way of mountain equipment and guidance. See 'What to buy'.

**Mountain Biking** is more and more popular and bikes are available for rent in Ambleside. This activity, which requires a level of fitness and stamina seldom apparent in the average tourist, has aroused controversy and there is regular conflict between walkers and mountain bikers. This is usually due to bikers using footpaths (where they are not allowed) instead of bridle paths. They usually pretend they didn't know they weren't allowed on footpaths, or they didn't know it was only a footpath, and this makes the walkers even madder. Most bikers don't help their cause by refusing to give any warning, by bell or otherwise, when they come flying up behind and past you. Apparently their current mindset is that only sissies put bells on their bikes.

## Armitt Museum & Library

'The Armitt' in Rydal Road houses a remarkable collection of historic tomes relevant to the district, available for reference, as well as artefacts of local interest. There is a Roman gravestone found near Galava fort, and a first edition of the King James

DO YOU MIND AWFULLY USING YOUR BELL?

Bible, known locally as the 'Curates Bible' because of the notes in its margins made by the curates of the old St Anne's Chapel. It was acquired in 1611, but disappeared towards the end of the seventeenth century. Reappearing 200 years later in Bradford, it was bought by local landowner and benefactor Colonel Rhodes who, it was expected, would donate it to the church. He didn't. On his death in 1905 it was acquired by a group of parishioners, including Mary Louisa Armitt, founder of this Library, and given to the parish church, which has now passed it to the library for safe keeping.

In addition, the Armitt has a collection of paintings by the avant-garde artist Kurt Schwitters who lived in Ambleside for a couple of years after World War Two, of whom more later.

A lesser known side of Beatrix Potter can also be found at the Armitt – her remarkable botanical paintings. She was an early member of the library and bequeathed these to it together with her first edition copies of her children's books.

## Annual Events

If you come in summer, Ambleside and district hosts some traditional annual events, including Ambleside Sports (which includes wrestling, hound trailing and athletics), country shows, Rydal sheep dog trials and the famous Rushbearing ceremony. In spring and autumn, the talented members of Ambleside Players produce traditional amateur theatrical entertainment, and you will find occasional musical recitals, often by well-known pianists, small orchestral groups and choirs. The long established 'Lake District Summer Music' performs some of its concerts here in August. In September 2016 a new four day event 'Festival of the Fells' was organised, combining the adventure activities offered by various outdoor interests, including films and talks, which it is expected will become an annual fixture. In November we have the spectacular Christmas Lights and Lantern procession.

SHOPPING IN AMBLESIDE

## What to Buy – Shopping

To repeat, Ambleside (once dubbed "Anorak Capital of the World") is home to very few "High Street" chain stores, although these are stealthily creeping in. Instead, you will find an amazing variety of individual shops, some of them specialising in uniquely local products, including foods, drinks, toiletries, slate ornaments, and original or reproduction watercolours of the famously beautiful Lakeland landscape as well as original works by contemporary painters, sculptors and potters. And if you need outdoor clothing, wait till you get to Ambleside! At the last count there were 16 retail outlets specialising in the great outdoors, which means that you can probably find a better choice of outdoor clothing here than you can anywhere else.

In Ambleside is the Lake District's largest garden centre, Hayes Garden World on Lake Road. It is a major employer and a huge attraction with a vast stock of everything horticultural and also a cafe, local foods, clothing, kitchen equipment and ornaments.

To support local craftspeople, look for quality gifts and mementos bearing the Made in Cumbria logo.

# Getting Around

Despite all kinds of persuasion, cajoling and sometimes active discouragement of motorists by the local authorities, the car remains the ideal and most popular way of getting around the area, making it possible to stay in one place and make daily excursions. The Lake District contains a thousand destinations of interest, from the start of classic walks and climbs to its great houses, churches, galleries and museums. Ambleside is no more than one hour's scenic drive away from any one of them. Outside the main urban centres, few of these destinations are adequately served by public transport, which is infrequent and expensive unless you are senior enough to have a bus pass. Park & Ride schemes don't exist.

A downside of this is that three cash strapped statutory bodies control parking and regard motorists as fair game to get their share of the tourism pot. You will not like the charges.

However, for the car-less and the car-haters, things are getting slowly better and it is possible to plan many enjoyable excursions by bus and on foot. Free passes for those eligible fill buses (after 9.30am), sometimes to the extent that local shoppers from outlying villages can't get home again. Where you can go by car, you can also go by bike, if you like plenty of exhilarating hills and don't mind mixing it on narrow roads with the buses and the cars. Safer biking routes are being developed and maps are available locally.

## Parking in Ambleside - easy!

**Off-street Car Parks** Ambleside has five 'Pay & Display' town centre car parks:

**Rydal Road** - a large long-stay car park on the left as you leave the town centre northwards towards Keswick or as you enter the town from Keswick.

**University campus, Rydal Road** – oppositethe Rydal Road car park.

**Lake Road** - as you go south from the centre (entrance on right just past 'Adventure Peaks').

**Low Fold** going south on Lake Road on the left

**Kelsick Road** - a short-stay (cheaper) car park opposite the Public Library.

Rothay Road, Miller Field – on left as you enter the town centre from the south.

Also Ambleside School, Vicarage Road – (after 5.00pm on school days) – donation boxes, don't be mean.

## On-street Parking

There are quite a lot of on-street parking spaces in the town centre. Parking control is operated by Cumbria County Council, not the Police. Council 'parking enforcement officers', unlike the Police, have nothing else to do so are more likely to catch you if you park illegally. If you park on the street in the town centre area between 10am and 6pm, your time is limited usually to one hour and you have to display the time you arrived, usually by means of a disc. This makes it easier for the wardens to nick you and interestingly forces you to be an accomplice in your own downfall.

You can get a disc free from local shops, Library and the Post Office/Tourist Info Centre, sometimes. If you have a disc from elsewhere it will do.

'I'M NOT PAYING TO PARK'

If you don't display your time of arrival in the town centre area between 10am and 6pm you could be nicked even if you have only been there 10 minutes, which is the time allowed for you to obtain a disc. Parking fines are currently £25 if paid early, double if not. If you can't get a disc, write and display your time of arrival on a piece paper.

Outside the town centre there are residential streets where parking is allowed but the on-street spaces there are badly needed by local residents most of whom have no off-street parking. This doesn't stop many tourists from parking outside houses and going on an all-day walk or even leaving a car for several days. If you know anyone who does this, it would help local/tourist relations if you asked them not do it again.

## Long term parking

There is no provision in public car parks for stays over 24 hours. There is a short stretch of the main A591 road south on the left just before Waterhead where you can park indefinitely. This is a mile out of the town centre.

## For your convenience:

Public toilets can be found at the Old Market Hall, at Rydal Road Car Park, at Low Fold Car Park (Lake Road), in White Platts Recreation Ground and in Rothay Park (this latter is only open seasonally), also at Waterhead. You need to have a 20p coin with you to avoid disappointment or worse. This contributes directly to local Parish funds for civic improvement projects.

If you need a rest as you explore the town, we also have an amazing number of public benches. At the last count in autumn 2016 a survey by Ambleside Civic Trust (Google it) counted 119, many dedicated to departed relatives who loved the town. The Trust's website links to a location map and it notes for each bench the position, condition and the person whom it commemorates.

## The Weather

A lot of misinformation is issued about the weather in the Lake District. Generalised weather forecasts for the 'north west' of England are often wildly inaccurate for this area, where the weather pattern is heavily influenced by our mountains. We are in a micro climate where clouds form when they don't elsewhere, but also where our mountains can keep clouds at bay and shelter us from westerly winds. Nevertheless, it can rain – a lot. But the Irish saying is true here too – if you don't like the weather, wait a minute. It

# THE WEATHER FORECAST

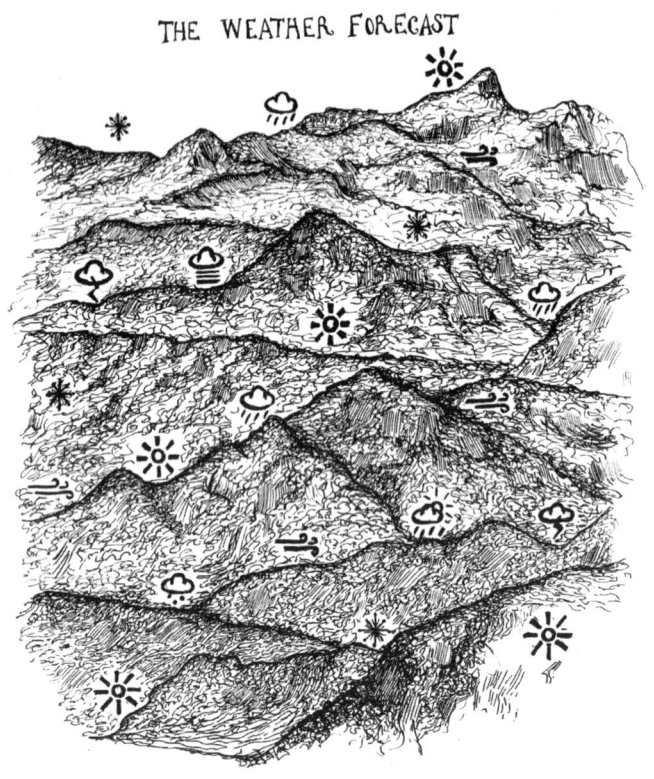

is very changeable, and although long periods of wet weather do occur, these are rare. Recent changes in global weather patterns seem to have favoured the Lake District with warmer, drier summers and mild winters. We are now a year-round tourist destination.

Hill walkers and climbers should go online to the National Park Weather Service for expected felltop conditions, temperatures, cloud base, etc.

The best advice is not to let weather stop you. Get some basic waterproofs and enjoy one or two walks in the rain! Rainbows are common and there's always a pub not far away, where boots and anoraks are welcome, and probably a real fire in winter. Expect sunshine too. After rain, nothing is more beautiful than the lush valleys and the tumbling becks glinting in the sunlight! It is while the weather changes from cloudy to clear that the real drama of the Lakeland landscape can be experienced.

## Weather tales

Local farmer to an American tourist, who asked whether it rained all the time: *"Well, it donks an' it doddles, dozzles bedoes, and mebbe it come a bit o' a stickter, but nivver what you might call a gay gurt pell!"*

And from Ambleside Oral Archive, interviewee John Wright, born 1923, interviewed 1993:

"Well, I allus remember going to Coniston on a pouring wet day, and I said to an old gentleman called Linnie Dixon, 'When is it going to stop raining, Linnie? Dreadful!' And he says 'It'll stop raining when the lake finds its level. If it goes down low in the summer, once it does rain it usually rains till the lake finds its own level.' And I said 'Well it's not high yet, so it's a bit to go.' And he said 'Yes well, it will, as soon as it finds its level it'll stop.'"

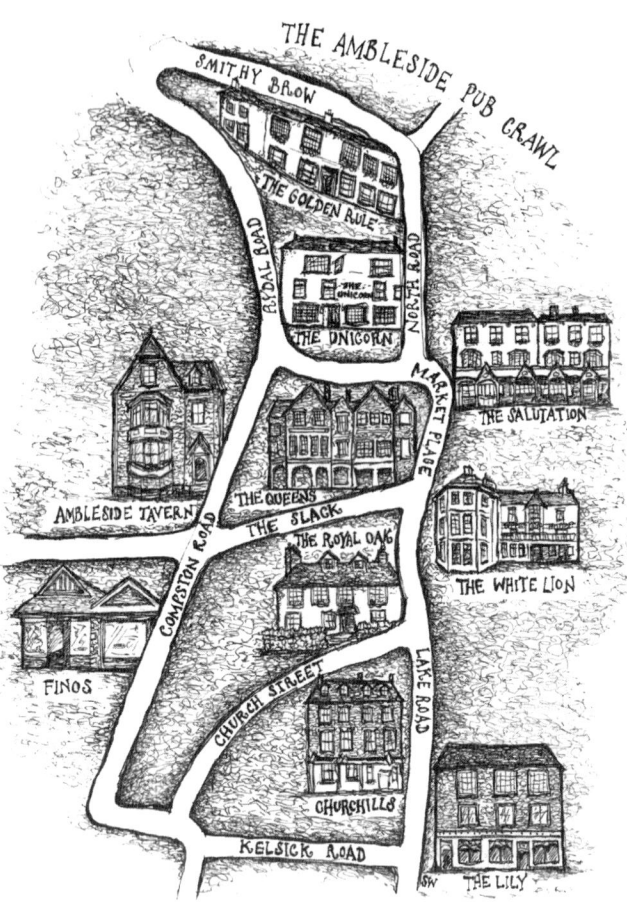

THE AMBLESIDE PUB CRAWL

SMITHY BROW

"THE GOLDEN RULE"

BYDAL ROAD

NORTH ROAD

THE UNICORN

THE SALUTATION

MARKET PLACE

AMBLESIDE TAVERN

THE QUEENS

COMBSTON ROAD

THE SLACK

THE ROYAL OAK

THE WHITE LION

FINOS

CHURCH STREET

LAKE ROAD

CHURCHILLS

KELSICK ROAD

THE LILY

# CHAPTER 3

# A walking tour of Ambleside's pubs and bars

History books tell us that there were five pubs in Rydal once, and two or three in Clappersgate. If you wonder where they were, thinking in terms of today's pubs, you would find that hard to believe. But it's true.

Lots of people lived in Rydal. There were five farms, three mills and a smithy, plus the Hall. And a pub in times past was perhaps simply the front room of a worker's cottage. After the 1830 Act which allowed anyone to brew beer, it would be the woman of the house who did the brewing.

In Ambleside it would have been the five pubs which still exist that supplied the town's drinking needs, which apparently were as considerable as they are today. The Golden Rule, Unicorn, Queens, White Lion and Royal Oak have all been there for centuries, probably pre-dated by the Salutation. Those that provided accommodation called themselves hotels. The Golden

Rule and the Royal Oak do not nowadays provide accommodation. More recent pubs are Churchills, previously a temperance hotel called the Vale View, the Ambleside Tavern, which older residents remember as the Copper Coins café and later the Sportsman, and The Lily. What follows is what we hope is a fair idea of what to expect.

The town centre pubs/bars are all within 5 minutes' walk of each other. There is a mix of free and tied houses. Cumbria as a whole has spawned a large number of microbreweries and most Ambleside pubs offer a selection of real ales from these thriving enterprises. Dozens of real ales are available. The pubs vary from quiet houses to busy places of entertainment. Live music is often played and some run quiz nights and bingo. Nearly all pubs offer all day food. Ambleside is a peaceful town and there is seldom any trouble in our pubs. A Barwatch scheme operates to deter the more excitable drinkers. Seriously bad behaviour gets you barred indefinitely from all local pubs. Our brief tour starts at the southern end of the town centre, in Lake Road.

**The Lily** – Located in Lake Road, on the left going south, this independent is the town's newest pub. Modern decor attracts all ages but mainly a younger crowd. The Lily offers several lagers, draught cider, some real ales and an extensive menu of starters, mains and light bites. Entertainments include Open mic on Sundays, speed quiz, comedy nights, live bands. Wi-Fi. There is no TV or sport.

**Churchills** – Turn right out of the Lily and Churchills is just a step away across the road. Once a temperance hotel, now a free house, this spacious pub appeals mainly to young people seeking entertainments with their drinks. Strong on Sky and BBC live sports transmissions, mainly football, Churchills also provides main meals and lite bites all day, karaoke, pool, a Bingo night, a Quiz night and Sunday roasts. There are two bars, Winston's at street level and a smaller one, Monty's, downstairs. At the bar is a large selection of lagers, ciders and some real ale. Wi-Fi. Rooms available for Bed & Breakfast.

**Royal Oak** – Turn left out of Churchills, 'The Oak' is on the corner of Lake Road and Church Street. This is an ancient traditional 17th century Lake District pub now owned by the John Barras company, popular with locals. Ceiling beams and real fire. Smallish rooms lend a cosy atmosphere. There is an attractive street corner outdoor area, sheltered and heated. A changing selection of mainly local real ales is available, also Guinness, lager, traditional draught ciders. Food offerings include pies, burgers, hot dogs, sandwiches and baguettes. Quiz and curry nights, some live music.

**White Lion Hotel** – Across Lake Road is the large White Lion with extensive outdoor table area, umbrellas and heaters when needed. Inside, the bar area is spacious, with an equally spacious dining area beyond. The bar serves an extensive real ale range, some local, with a 'try before you buy' option, and discount for CAMRA members. There is an extensive food menu of starters, sharers, pasta, pub classics. There are 7 bedrooms.

**Queen's Hotel** – Almost opposite in Market Place is the Queen's. This has a long history, being used once as a youth hostel and as a refuge for the evacuated Royal College of Art during WW2. There is a large bar and dining area. The range of well-kept real ales is extensive, local and reasonably priced. The extensive food list includes steaks, pies and roasts. The warren-like Cellar bar downstairs has a range of lagers and shows football on TV. Music downstairs is provided by a juke box and there is a free pool table. A small tree shaded patio can be accessed from both bars for smokers and a TV monitor is viewable there. Dog friendly in the bar. Wi-Fi. Twenty six bedrooms for B&B.

**Ambleside Tavern** – Leaving the Queens by either exit, go left, past the shopping precinct and left again at the traffic lights into Compston Road,. Ambleside Tavern (previously known as The Sportsman) is across the road on the right. This is a Thwaites Brewery house offering their range of real ales plus changing local ones. Bar meals are available, including starters and mains, burgers and ciabattas. Sky and BT sport on TV. Live music on

Saturdays. In the cellar downstairs there is sometimes a late disco on Fridays and Saturdays. Dogs welcome. Wi-Fi.

**Fino Wine Bar** – Turn right out of the Tavern, right again at the cinema and Fino is opposite, next to the Walnut chippy. This quiet small bar offers good quality wines, cocktails, beers and also spirits from the Lakes Distillery. 'Sharing boards' of local cheeses and good quality charcuterie are available to accompany drinks.

**Unicorn Inn** – If you can still walk safely, retrace your steps up past the Tavern, turn right at the traffic lights, past the shopping precinct and turn first left into North Road, once the main route through the town. On the left is the Unicorn, a Robinson's Brewery pub serving only Robinson's real ales, plus Guinness, lagers and draught cider. This is a historic 400 year old traditional small Lakeland house with a cosy and friendly atmosphere, popular with visitors for its live music (Thursdays and Saturdays) with a folk and country flavour. Open mic possible on Saturdays. Food is served lunchtimes (12 till 2) and evenings (5 till 9) and there is a good home cooked menu. Wi-Fi. Football on TV. Five bedrooms are let for B&B.

**Golden Rule** – Leaving the Unicorn, turn left up North Road and go first left into the Golden Rule by the back yard, where there is plenty of outdoor seating, some covered and heated. This is a historic Lakeland Robinson's (previously Hartleys) pub serving only Robinson's real ales of which there is an extensive choice. Also served are lagers and draught ciders. There are four rooms, beams and real fire. The pub has had the same landlord since 1981. He has steadfastly resisted attempts to introduce food, sports TV and music (although good pork pies, scotch eggs and packet snacks are available). As such the pub is very popular with those who seek a peaceful atmosphere where quiet sociable conversation is preferred to music and other distractions. Darts. Wi-Fi. Dog friendly.

**Ambleside Salutation** – Very much a hotel rather than a pub, the 'Sally' has an excellent lounge bar, comfortable, quiet and sedate, with a fine bar and restaurant menu. Non-residents are welcome.

**Badger Bar** – Out at Rydal (mile and a half north on the A591, see 'easy walks' page) the Badger Bar is part of the Glen Rothay Hotel. Friendly and very popular with walkers, it has a bar room, dining room and a large outdoor seating area adjacent to the road. It serves a selection of locally brewed real ales and a bar menu. At the time of writing an unusual feature is the regular evening feeding of badgers, who descend quite tamely from the woods above, making it quite literally a badger bar. (So far they have not been allowed inside and badger is not on the menu.)

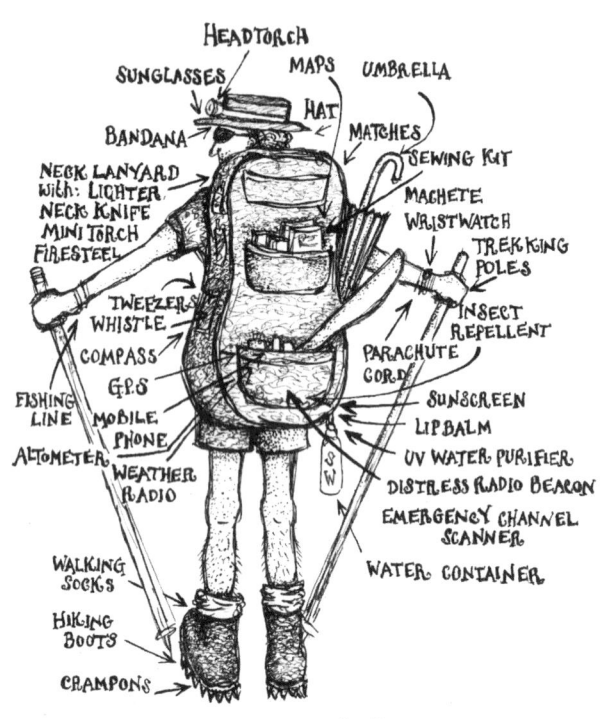

HEADTORCH

SUNGLASSES    MAPS    UMBRELLA

BANDANA    HAT
                    MATCHES

NECK LANYARD
with: LIGHTER    SEWING KIT
NECK KNIFE    MACHETE
MINI TORCH    WRISTWATCH
FIRESTEEL    TREKKING
                    POLES

TWEEZERS
WHISTLE    INSECT
                    REPELLENT
COMPASS    PARACHUTE
G.P.S    CORD
FISHING    SUNSCREEN
LINE    MOBILE    LIP BALM
PHONE
ALTOMETER    UV WATER PURIFIER
    WEATHER    DISTRESS RADIO BEACON
    RADIO    EMERGENCY CHANNEL
                    SCANNER
WALKING    WATER CONTAINER
SOCKS

HIKING
BOOTS

CRAMPONS →

THE PREPARED WALKER

# CHAPTER 4

# Walking routes from Ambleside

There was a time when visitors to the Lake District read Baddeley's guide book, bought a 1 inch OS map and set off into the hills wearing whatever clothes they had, a pair of wellies perhaps, an old mac, a tweed cap and jacket and an umbrella. Nearly all of them survived and enjoyed their adventures. They only came in summer.

Then came Wainwright, organised mountain rescue and dire warnings about safety, hi-tech outdoor clothing, ergonomic rucksacks, Gore-Tex lined boots, leki poles, GPS and mobile phones. With these also came crowds, outdoor gear shops, guided walks, fanatical peak baggers and footpath erosion. It is quite common now to see people on Loughrigg (20 minutes easy walk from the town centre) wearing and carrying hundreds of pounds worth of kit good enough to survive winter in the Himalayas, often in groups of 20 or more, treading away the thin soggy winter grass.

We mention this from the viewpoint of an older generation with the benefit of a well developed, if possibly subversive, sense of proportion and a preference for the way some things used to be.

From being something local shepherds did when they had no option, hill walking has become a passion for some, a reason for living for others, an exhilarating pleasure, a status booster or something to be carefully avoided in favour of a few pints by the pub fire.

The above comments aside, there are risks on the hills especially outside the summer season. Get aware of the sensible precautions to take. Read the 'STAY SAFE' page on the Langdale/Ambleside MRT's website. Do not rely solely on battery powered electronics!

If you are taking a dog on the fells off a lead and it is not sheep trained, it will chase sheep. If it does this, farmers are legally entitled to shoot your dog and may well do so especially if their ewes are in lamb. Cows with calves will normally not bother you but they will attack any dog that comes too close. If the dog is on a lead, the cows will probably attack you too. If you are approached menacingly, let your dog go!

## Easy Walks From Ambleside

Leaflets illustrating the following and similar walks are available from shops and the Tourist Information Centre/Post Office. Someone recently said there are 23 walks starting in Ambleside, though what they classed as a walk isn't known.

# From Ambleside to Grasmere via Rydal

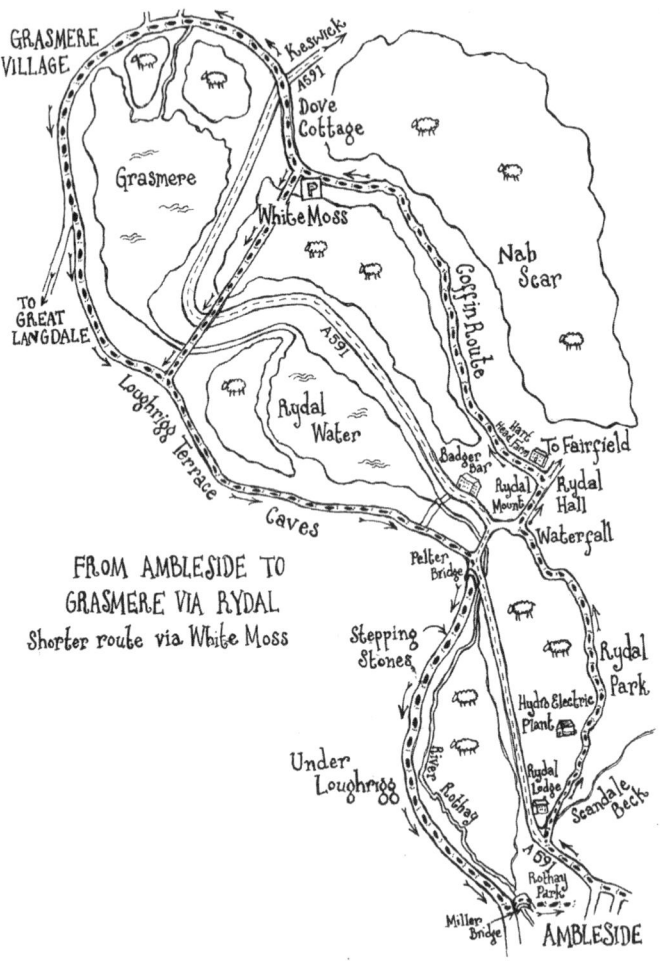

GRASMERE VILLAGE

To Keswick A591

Dove Cottage

Grasmere

White Moss

P

Nab Scar

TO GREAT LANGDALE

Coffin Route

Loughrigg Terrace

Rydal Water

A591

Caves

Hart Head Farm

To Fairfield

Badger Bar

Rydal Mount

Rydal Hall

Waterfall

FROM AMBLESIDE TO
GRASMERE VIA RYDAL
Shorter route via White Moss

Pelter Bridge

Stepping Stones

Under Loughrigg

River Rothay

Hydro Electric Plant

Rydal Park

Rydal Lodge

Scandale Beck

A591

Rothay Park

Miller Bridge

AMBLESIDE

This gentle walk takes you from the A591 just north of the town, through Rydal Park and Rydal Hall to the old 'coffin road', which runs from the back of Rydal Mount giving good views over Rydal Water, ending at Dove Cottage, thence into Grasmere village. You can take in Dora's Field at Rydal too, so it's very Wordsworth. Once in Grasmere either catch a bus back to Ambleside or turn left at the church and continue along Red Bank Road, past Fairy Glen (refeshments in season) to the first stile on the left, drop down to the lake and follow the shore path. At the lake end, follow the Terrace Short of Grasmere, you can drop down to White Moss at the north end of Rydal Water, crossing the footbridge over the Rothay, through the woods to the open fell and return to Ambleside round the far side of the lake, visiting 'Rydal Cave', a spectacular old quarry working, and then following the Underloughrigg road. There are no serious uphill pulls on this route.

TROUTBECK OVER WANSFELL

# Troutbeck over Wansfell

This walk is not long but is strenuous for the first half hour or so, involving the steep walk up the side of Wansfell, the fell overlooking Ambleside to the east. You start up the lane behind the Salutation Hotel. A mile or so up the lane, out on to the open meadow, a stile straddles the wall on your right to commence the climb. On reaching the top, it is downhill all the way to Troutbeck village, via Nanny Lane. Turn right on to the road and right again at the Post Office to return to Ambleside through farm land and woods round the southern flank of Wansfell via Jenkyn's Crag, a fine viewpoint over Windermere. The walk can be done in reverse of course, avoiding the steep uphill to Wansfell top. You get the steep downhill instead. A shorter variation on this is to turn right at the top of Wansfell and follow a path due south, which will bring you down near Jenkyn's Crag.

## Underloughrigg and Rydal Park

This is a really soft walk with virtually no ascent. It is ideally suited to those recuperating from heart attacks, violent hangovers or loss of a leg. Start down Vicarage Road, go straight through Rothay Park, over the arched Miller Bridge, turn right and carry on walking for a mile and a half. You will pass Fox How, once the home of Matthew Arnold, and the picturesque stepping stones across the River Rothay. Cross Pelter Bridge, where the artist Fred Yates met future US president Woodrow

Wilson, and turn left on to the main road. After 200 yards turn right up the road towards Rydal Mount. In springtime it's worth going through the churchyard to Dora's Field to see the daffodils Wordsworth planted in memory of his daughter. Continue up the road to Rydal Mount where you can stop and visit the house, Wordsworth's home for many years. Opposite side of the lane is Rydal Hall, now a religious conference centre. Go through the Hall gateway. A gate on the right opens into the formal gardens, well worth a look. Then exit through a door in the wall and continue to the bridge which crosses Rydal Beck. Look left and right at the lovely falls and maybe visit the ancient Grot viewpoint (see info on site). Then if you're there at the right time you can get tea and buns from the Hall café. Keep walking and you will emerge on to the main A591 at Rydal Lodge where you turn left back into town.

## Loughrigg including Lily Tarn and Todd Crag

Loughrigg is a low but delightful fell, stretching all the way from above Ambleside to above Grasmere. From its heights you can choose a variety of routes

# Loughrigg including Lily Tarn and Todd Crag

down – to Loughrigg Tarn, thence to Elterwater, or Skelwith Bridge and waterfall, or to Rydal Water, or Grasmere lake. The southern end of Loughrigg is a fine rocky summit known as Todd Crag with a brilliant view of the town, Waterhead and the whole of Windermere lake. It takes less than half an hour on average from Ambleside to the top, via Vicarage Road, Rothay Park, over the bridge, turn right, over the cattle grid, turn left over another cattle grid, steepish up to the houses, then up the wall steps, through the stile, and take either the path ahead or up to the right. Either will bring you to Todd Crag, the one to the right passing Lily Tarn. Once there, Loughrigg is a good place to just wander. To the north the summit and trig point offer views to Grasmere and the Langdale valleys.

There is local joke about locals getting lost on Loughrigg, as if you've got to be daft to do so. In reality it is easy to get disorientated there in mist or low cloud as one of the many paths looks much like another.

## Round Hill, Grove Farm and Stock Ghyll Force

This is a short afternoon walk into the hills approaching Kirkstone Pass, to which you could continue. Leave Ambleside by North Road, into Kirkstone Road and turn left up Sweden Bridge Lane. Take the second right (Ellerigg Road) and at the top turn right on to the footpath taking you through Thistly Wood. This emerges on to the Kirkstone Road. Turn left here,

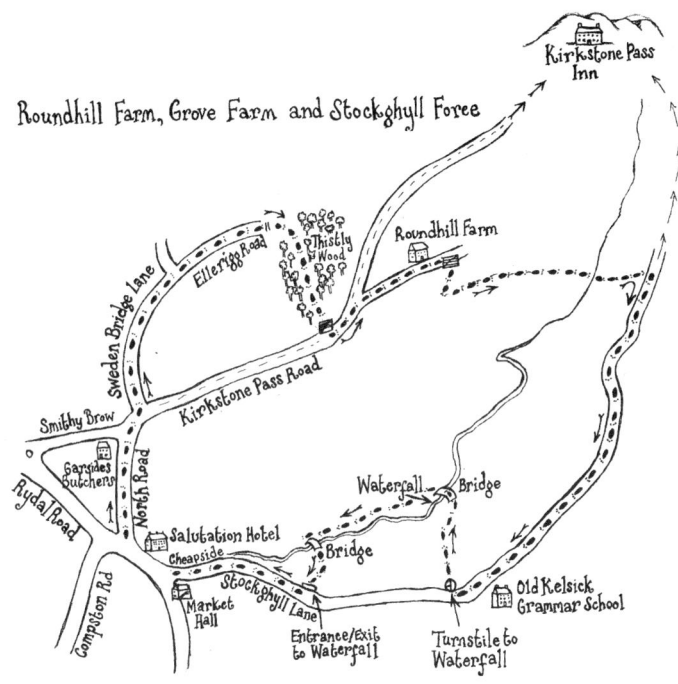

Roundhill Farm, Grove Farm and Stockghyll Force

past the cottages on the right, then first right down the track to Round Hill Farm. At the farm go through the stile on the right and follow the zigzag path down into the valley, cross by the bridge and walk towards Grove Farm. When you reach tarmac, turn right to go back to town along the flank of Wansfell. On the way back go through the old turnstile gate on the right into Stock Ghyll Park for a look at the beautiful waterfalls.

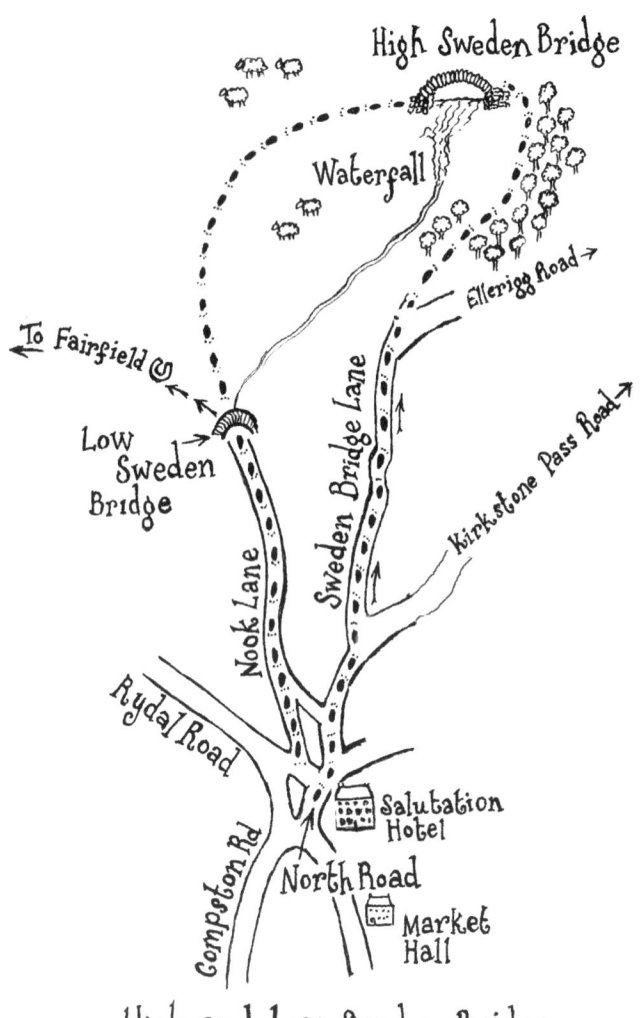

High and Low Sweden Bridge

# High and Low Sweden Bridge

This is a short uphill stroll from Ambleside, less than 2 miles, to a lovely little packhorse type bridge over Scandale Beck above a little waterfall. (The path beyond the bridge leads up to Scandale and eventually out on to Red Screes or Dove Crag but these are more strenuous walks.) Take the same route out of town as the previous walk, but instead of turning right into Ellerigg Road, go straight on. The road becomes a track. Just keep going till you reach the bridge, which is a restful and picturesque picnic spot. You can come back the same way, but if you cross the bridge and cut up to the left along a wall you will soon find the track which goes right to High Pike and Fairfield (another long high walk). But turn left on this track to return to town via Low Sweden Bridge, through the farm yard and down Nook Lane.

## Waterhead via River Rothay

An even softer level walk which might appeal to families with young children is to set off into Rothay Park via Vicarage Road. As soon as you enter the park, veer leftish past the playground to an obvious path which brings you out by the Football Club pavilion. Go left, then right through the car park leaving by the vehicle exit. Go alongside the bowling green and turn right on the road. Cross carefully (the one-way road is busy) to the pavement and follow round. At the second (main) entrance to Rothay Manor Hotel, carefully cross the road and go right through a gate adjacent to the Woolly Rug Company premises. Don't go over the footbridge, go left and follow the riverside path all the way into Galava field with its remains of the Roman fort. Take the usual precautions if there are cows with calves, then go through the cast iron kissing gate into Borrans Park. Here you can play on the lake shore before continuing to Waterhead promenade where there are all kinds of goodies, including the Waterhead Hotel garden with outdoor pizza oven, the choc dip ice cream and coffee shop, gift shops, boats for hire and the Pier for the café and lake cruises. A little further on is the Youth Hostel with lake shore, bar and café open to non-residents.

# Strenuous Full To Half Day Walks from Ambleside

The following walks are described in detail on John Dawson's Lake District Walks website (www.lakedistrictwalks.com).

## Loughrigg, Sergeant Man and Tarn Crag

White Moss – Loughrigg (via caves) – Silver How – Blea Rigg – Sergeant Man – Tarn Crag – Grasmere – White Moss (Grid ref. NY 348066).

This walk starts from the A591 White Moss car parks at Rydal, takes you high above Grasmere towards the Langdale Pikes and back via Easedale.

Total Distance 12.1 miles, Total Ascent 3300 feet, Equivalent Distance 18.8 miles.

## The Langdale Pikes and Sergeant Man

New Dungeon Ghyll – Loft Crag – Pike o'Stickle – Harrison Stickle – Pavey Ark – Thunacar Knott – High Raise – Sergeant Man – Blea Rigg – New Dungeon Ghyll (Grid ref. NY 296064).

This walk starts in Great Langdale, takes you up to the Langdale Pikes and back, including a couple of other nearby summits.

Total Distance 6.5 miles, Total Ascent 3400 feet, Equivalent Distance 13.2 miles.

## Red Screes & Dove Crag

Ambleside - Red Screes - Little Hart Crag - Dove Crag - High Pike - Ambleside (Grid ref. NY 377046).

Starting at the town centre, this walk takes you into the high fells north of Ambleside, eventually giving fine views of Ullswater and the Helvellyn range, and Windermere as you return.

Total Distance 9.5 miles, Total Ascent 3500 feet, Equivalent Distance 16.6 miles.

## Fairfield Horseshoe

Ambleside - Nab Scar - Heron Pike - Great Rigg - Fairfield - Hart Crag - Dove Crag - High Pike - Ambleside (Grid ref. NY 377046).

This is perhaps the best known and most popular long walk from Ambleside, giving similar views northwards as the Red Screes walk. This version is clockwise, ascending steep Nab Scar first. A lot of people do the route anti-clockwise, either way it's a great walk. There is in places no discernible footpath on the bare tops of Fairfield and Hart Crag and it is quite easy to lose your way in cloud, ending up anywhere from Grasmere to Patterdale. This is no reason not to do the walk – just take care and a compass.

Total Distance 10.1 miles, Total Ascent 3100 feet, Equivalent Distance 16.4 miles.

## Scafell Pike from Langdale

Old Dungeon Ghyll – Rossett Gill – Esk Hause – Scafell Pike – Great End – Esk Pike – Bowfell – Three Tarns – Old Dungeon Ghyll (Grid ref. NY 286060).

Bag England's highest peak and see some the Lake District's famous rock climbing crags.

Total Distance 11.2 miles, Total Ascent 4600 feet, Equivalent Distance 20.4 miles

# Mountain Rescue

The Langdale/Ambleside Mountain Rescue Team is a major institution in the town. It is one of eleven teams in Cumbria and is the busiest in the country. Around 40 dedicated and highly trained members answer around a hundred calls for help every year. They are very well organised and equipped, and experts in telecoms and computer aided logistics in this difficult terrain. Many members are very fit, taking part in local mountain extreme sports, of which more later. They are highly trained in mountaineering and paramedical techniques.

In recent years, as climate change has brought unprecedented winter storms and flooding to the area, the team has willingly used its expertise to help the community cope with the emergencies which result. Its Landrovers are adapted to cope with flood waters as well as snow, ice and steep terrain. More recently team members have received training in swift river rescue. At the time of writing our local ambulance base has not been restored following flood damage and the rescue team base in Lake Road is hosting the ambulance service.

WHAT DOES SHE BLOODY EXPECT WEARING JIMMY CHOOS!?!

The team's website (**www.lamrt.org.uk**) comprehensively covers its activities, call-outs, personnel, and offers safety advice for those venturing into the hills, advice which if followed by more people might reduce the team's workload. If you have a look at the incidents attended by the team, human folly or culpable ignorance is at the root of many mountain disasters. To their credit, the team never apportions blame, even when their own lives may have been put at risk by others' stupidity.

To be a team member requires dedication - to fitness, training and acquiring expertise in advanced life saving techniques. Officials need organisational, administrative and IT expertise. Fund raising is an ongoing exercise as by choice the teams prefer the independence which self-funding gives. Not for them any control or bureaucratic interference from officialdom.

So being a team member is not something you can do casually, although it was in the early days. Ambleside Oral History Archive has some accounts of past impromptu improvisations such as using five bar gates for stretchers and pigsties or earth closets for storing the bodies of fallen rock climbers awaiting the coroner's arrival. At one time in the not too distant past some local doctors were so enthusiastically involved as team members that it was said that the quickest way to get to see a doctor was to collapse half way up a mountain.

In 2015 the team attended 127 incidents and members logged over 4100 hours in action. Eighty-eight of the incidents involved fellwalking, with lower leg injuries and getting lost forming the majority of these. They dealt with five fatalities. Helicopter evacuation of casualties is sometimes used when necessary but it is not always available.

Team members are all volunteers and rely on public support for finance. There is no money in it for them, which begs the question – what motivates them? A love of mountains, adventure, the adrenalin rushes, the drama, an empathy with mountain users? A wish to be a hero, to get a bit of glory? An excuse to get out of the house? A genuine desire to assist those in trouble or danger? The camaraderie of being part of a useful efficient and respected team? We suspect it is some or several of these things. Or something else. Whatever it is, we are thankful and proud they are doing what they do. They are grateful to the late Ada Hillard, of former Hillards Supermarkets which was bought out by Tesco in 1987 for £220 million. Ada settled in Ambleside and was a benefactor for several local institutions. She part funded the Rescue Team's headquarters.

# St John's Ambulance

St John's Ambulance has a base in Ambleside. Older members have memories of earlier days when there was no County Ambulance Service and St John's carried out the roles of the present service and also mountain rescue before the formation of specialist teams. Tales of dramatic and amusing incidents can be found on Ambleside Oral Archive's website.

From Ambleside Oral Archive – interviewee Cecil Otway, born 1910, interviewed 1985:

> But if we ran a rummage sale, in those days and made £12 or £13, we thought we'd done wonderfully well. Then we used to always have an August Monday, was our parade day. A big parade day. We had all sorts of sports, coconut shies, down in the park in those days. In Rothay Park? Yes, that was quite a big do, wasn't it. That's when I broke my arm. How did you break your arm? Winding the ambulance van up, and it back-fired and broke my arm. That was in 1932. Did your colleagues come and give you first aid? Oh yes, everybody down there thought it was a mock accident but it was a real one.

# CHAPTER 5

# The community today – the issues, the factions and the feuds

Eight kinds of people live around here:

## 1. Those who were born here

These are mostly grand folk. They still have the vendetta and they have a bush telegraph which makes the internet look pathetic. They are seldom academic, but don't let this fool you into thinking they are daft. Bred from a long tradition of survival in what was a hostile and isolated place, they just prefer to concentrate on the practicalities of life. There is no modern technology they cannot master. Also they will weigh you up in a trice and treat you with courtesy despite what they think of you. If you should happen to engage one in conversation and ask if they've lived here all their life, they will possibly answer "Not yet", which would of course be entirely correct.

Charles Dickens made some rude comments about the apparently excessive drinking habits of the local people. The only thing that has changed is that there are more locals now. One theory is that this drinking is stress related, brought on by constant territorial invasion by tourists.

## 2. Those who run tourist businesses

These are the ones who will take your money, and they include some from above and some tourists who wouldn't go home. They are like small businessmen everywhere. They always have a bad season and always buy a new car every year and go on at least one long-haul holiday. Within the community, however, they are generous to a fault. Ambleside is famous for its support of charities and these people are second to none in giving. They give away goods for prizes, they give donations, they give their precious time (out of main season). The jobs they provide are almost all we've got.

## 3. Those who work for the above

Some of these were born here and have English as a native language, although if you are a southerner you might find some of the Poles easier to understand. Or the Czechs, but maybe not the Bulgarians, Hungarians and Romanians. Many of these hard working folk enjoy minimum wages, zero hours contracts if any, zero job security and live in multi-occupancy bedsit houses. So err on the side of tolerance when they get your order wrong – they're not paid enough to have to put up with histrionics from over-demanding customers.

## 4. Those who came here to die

These are a mixture. They have time on their hands, if not on their side. Some are totally brilliant. They do voluntary work and the brainy ones join the University of the Third Age. Some of them are community minded, which is good. Others are very concerned to "protect" the area and do the National Park Authority's job for it. They derive their income from elsewhere and some of them would like tourism to contract to the point where they didn't notice it, regardless of the effect on others' livelihoods. They campaign for olde worlde lamp posts and the restoration of slippery cobbles, and they idealise the Lake District of 150 years ago when lots of locals were starving, emigrating and living till they were 40.

## 5. Tourists

These are the lifeblood of the town and we are glad they continue to arrive. We also sometimes wish they'd go away, such is the lot of those who can never call their territory their own. This contradiction causes us to have personality problems. Tourists are made very welcome except when they come in vast groups and all arrange to meet in the same tiny pub at the same time or when they dither about blocking our narrow pavements, especially annoying the increasing numbers of us using mobility scooters. We nevertheless work very hard to give them what they like in the way of food, accommodation and things to take home. They sometimes ask silly questions, which makes our day. Like "Is this the ferry for the Isle of Man?" at the lake pier, or "Where is Peter Rabbit's grave?". One, when asked if he'd seen the Langdale

Pikes, said "We haven't been fishing." They are all made very welcome, until they threaten to stay.

# 6. Offcomers

These include those in 3 above. Offcomers outnumber native locals by about four to one. It has to be said that offcomers now run the place and contribute mightily to the community. Others however are careless about respecting local customs and traditions. They commit offences against community heritage, like buying and changing the names of historic landmark buildings, such as is not allowed in some more sensible countries. Some others oppose changes which could be of benefit to the community, such as the development of new housing for local working people or new commercial developments which promise better jobs. Community is not a concept that they understand. The day may come when those self-centred nimbys find they have to go to Kendal or Lancaster for a plumber to fix their boilers because all the trades people can no longer afford to live here.

## 7. Students

These study outdoor education and some environmental stuff at the Ambleside campus of the **University of Cumbria** (previously St. Martins College, and Charlotte Mason College – see later) and live in the second homes which have been converted into bedsits by their absentee owners to pay the mortgage. Some work in pubs and cafés. Their nose and navel studs and sometimes their antisocial antics provoke comments like 'would you want that teaching your kids?' from locals who know from experience that some of them get to like Ambleside so much that they will remain here after their courses and try to get jobs or marry locals. They represent a welcome influx of fresh style and talent from outside the area.

## 8. Recent Immigrants

These are mainly from eastern Europe and Spain. The Spanish ones often move on quickly as they can't tolerate the weather. You've got to have more reasons than a poorly paid job to put up with the winter climate here. Many of the eastern Europeans (predominantly

## THE UNDERMINING OF COMMUNITY INTEGRITY

① HOLIDAY MAKERS BUY SECOND HOME

② INVESTORS OR BUSINESSES BUY HOUSES FOR HOLIDAY LETTING.

↘

COST OF HOUSING RISES DUE TO LIMITED HOUSING STOCK

↓

FAMILIES AND YOUNG PEOPLE FORCED OUT OF THE COMMUNITY DUE TO LACK OF ANY AFFORDABLE HOUSING

↓

AVERAGE AGE OF LOCAL POPULATION RISES

↓

VOLUNTEER BASE FOR IMPORTANT LOCAL NEEDS SUCH AS MOUNTAIN RESCUE, PARISH COUNCIL ETC DWINDLES

←

SCHOOLS AND LOCAL SERVICES SUFFER AS NOT ENOUGH LOCALS TO JUSTIFY PROVISION

↖

OLDER POPULATION NEEDS CARERS WHO CANNOT AFFORD TO LIVE HERE

↑

HOLIDAY AND SECOND HOME OWNERS EXERT INFLUENCE TO OPPOSE AFFORDABLE HOUSING FOR LOCALS

↑

NOW AMBLESIDE HAS 40% OF HOUSING NOT LIVED IN BY LOCAL OCCUPANTS AND IS NOT ALWAYS ABLE TO FILL COMMUNITY POSITIONS.

---

Poles) have been here for many years. They earn more in our low paid service industries than they can back home following the professions they are qualified for, such as lawyers, scientists, teachers and accountants. In their jobs here they are very reliable, polite and conscientious and thus much valued by local employers. Pay peanuts without getting monkeys!

The 2011 census revealed that 3.5% of the population of Ambleside and Grasmere spoke an eastern European language. In the five years since then, many more have arrived, but others have gone back home or elsewhere.

For the interested outside observer, it is useful to remember that most of these groupings dislike each other. If you imagine that you are going to find a haven here of peace and harmony among the tranquil valleys, forget it. Born and bred locals resent offcomers who prosper while they don't. Business interests resent the interference of those retired conservationists who try to influence amenity groups and the local councils in order to object to development. Some retired conservationists hate everyone who commits the sacrilege of trying to promote tourism in their chosen paradise. Some people smile with one face at the tourists as they take their money, and smirk at them with the other as the rain pours down, but most of us hope you have a really good time. So it's no different from where you live, unless you're holed up in a city and you don't even know what your neighbour looks like.

Despite the above comments, Ambleside is a caring community. If you've got social problems, temporary money or mobility troubles or need other support, Ambleside is not a bad place to be. But don't all rush! You may need to qualify! There is a core of caring people here who run social clubs for the elderly and the sick, visit the lonely or bereaved and report instances of hardship. And neighbours generally know and care about each other.

## Some Issues

These are many and are mainly caused by the eight categories of people above plus those who don't live here but think they know what's best for the Lake District. They really mean what's best for what they think the Lake District should be and they sometimes forget about those who actually live here and need to make a living.

### Here are some issues:

- Overpriced housing due to second and holiday home housing market (get a social conscience!)

- Dwindling population of young people and young families due to same cause high cost of living, due to high rates caused by inflated property values and lack of large discount retailers.

- No diversity of employment, due to draconian development restrictions, causing over-dependence on tourism with its usually low wage levels and unsocial working hours which disrupt family life, all causing talented young people and families to emigrate.

- Lack of adequate car parking, due to the National Park Authority's policy of making life difficult for motorists in case more come. (More still come.)

## Intrigues

- These are only four of many fascinating imponderables;

- Is it true that ewes are a temptation for virile shepherds in high and hidden places?

- Does cockfighting continue in lonely secret barns on wild dark nights?

- Is it true that unlawful liaisons (historically necessary in small isolated communities) still go on behind the closed doors of remote dwellings?

- Do badgers and squirrels form a significant part of the local diet?

WHAT CAN I DO FOR YOU TODAY DARLIN'

Regrettably, because of the insatiable desire of travel writers and promoters of tourism to turn every facet of Lakeland life into an Attraction, we cannot supply the answers to these questions. It is said, however, that the nearest thing yet to total chaos is Ambleside on Fathers' Day. Or was that Liverpool?

# The Health and Fitness of the Parish

Ambleside has a Health Centre, an optician and we even have an NHS dentist.

Concerned as always about the wellbeing of our community, we asked local GP Dr Paul Davies, a wild water swimmer, to give us an overview of our demographics, health and fitness. Are we top heavy with geriatrics? Have we a dearth of young people? Do we suffer any afflictions peculiar to the Lake District? Does our environment improve our chances of living forever? This is his response, for which we are in his debt – if we sell any copies of this book we will consider buying him a new skinny dipping costume.

## Here is Dr Davies' valuable contribution:

The population of Ambleside and the age profile of its residents are very interesting. The idea that there is a preponderance of elderly residents is not borne out by the actual statistics. Approximately 18% of people are 65 – 84 years old and 3% are 85 years or more and this is actually very similar to the population of South Cumbria generally, although these percentages are influenced by the current number of students at the Ambleside campus of the University of Cumbria.

Various local outdoor activities, indulged in frenetically at all hours of the day and night, may give the impression of an uber fit population – but is that the reality? Certainly many people of all ages walk and exercise regularly and Ambleside Athletic Club and the football and cricket clubs are thriving. But access to municipal sports facilities is limited. Kendal is the nearest public swimming pool, so you have to join a health club locally to enable your children to swim regularly, unless they enjoy the sometimes chilly challenge of local waters. Likewise, gym memberships are through local hotels but unfortunately teenagers are denied access to local gyms. (Too many of them misbehave). Local instructors lead fitness classes for old and young, and regular yoga and Pilates sessions are held in Ambleside throughout the year. Ambleside is fortunate in retaining its own Health Centre, with a long tradition of person and family centred General Practice administered by varied and eccentric Doctors and Nurse Practitioners committed to delivering holistic health care. Over the years the practice has specialised in providing trauma and minor injury care, minor surgery and General Practice in a rural setting, as Ambleside is an hour at least from a full accident and emergency unit. Within the practice are a comprehensive array of other practitioners with physiotherapy, chiropody, counselling and psychological therapy all on site. The practice also has a strong Mindfulness ethos, with GPs and other staff teaching this, or studying it as a course. They also provide medical care to over 3000 temporary residents, who are on holiday in the area and present with all manner of medical conditions, from simply forgetting their regular medication, to suffering acute heart attacks or strokes. It is often fascinating, challenging and satisfying treating people on holiday where their usual support systems do not exist - family pressures to recover rapidly (so as not to spoil everyone's holiday) often influence illness behaviour, although people tend to attend the surgery more on the rainy days of their holiday when resilience to their affliction can be modified by the weather. There are no unique medical conditions peculiar to Ambleside, although there are regular consultations from those with tick bites during the spring and summer and horse fly bites can be dramatic!! Many patients are quite stoical with their afflictions, or simply too busy working to attend surgery. Farmers in particular tend to persevere with often serious conditions where others would not. The prevalence of common diseases is similar to national levels, although there is an unexplained higher rate of cancer in South Lakes overall compared to national figures.

Many people work very hard in Ambleside running tourism related businesses and the idyllic notion of doing a few hours work then relaxing on the fells is far from reality for many. Split shifts, low wages, an ever longer tourism season and the uncertain financial climate cause a lot of psychological stresses as well as fatigue and exhaustion overall to hotel and restaurant workers and owners alike. Anxiety and depression levels are similar to those elsewhere in the country, although perhaps there is an added depression factor – when all around you are relaxing on holiday and apparently having a lovely time and you live in a beautiful area, it may be even harder to cope with depression. During the winter months of wetter, shorter days many people have proven low vitamin D levels, associated with the lack of sunlight. Supplements are now routinely advised.

Elderly residents can sometimes become relatively isolated when they get ill or simply infirm. They may have retired here from afar, leaving family support behind. Although there is a strong community spirit in Ambleside, not all incoming residents integrate socially into the village. There are no local residential or nursing homes, so that should such facilities be needed then older residents have to move away from any local friends or family into care homes nearer Kendal or elsewhere in South Lakes. Referral to specialists usually involves travel to Kendal, Lancaster or Barrow for assessment and treatment, which can present the elderly with travel difficulties. Likewise care agencies are stretched locally, with a wide geographical area to cover, competing employment and wage opportunities from local tourism businesses and the fact that carers are increasingly unable to afford to live locally.

The residents of Ambleside have a high expectation of health continuing into old age, with a generally very positive outlook, perhaps in contrast to lower expectations in more deprived, urban areas in Cumbria. Overall, elderly residents tend to enjoy a relatively healthy and active old age compared to other areas, and Ambleside is a compact village with essential amenities, although its narrow pavements can be clogged with tourists impeding the progress of any residents using a mobility scooter!!

As mentioned, Ambleside is at least an hour away from a full Accident & Emergency unit. Combined with the possibility of road congestion, this is not an ideal place to have a heart attack or stroke. However we have First Responders based locally and these are called out automatically if an ambulance is not near enough. They carry oxygen and defibrillators as well as other first aid items. We can also call on the Air Ambulance service which although based in Blackpool can get here in 15 minutes - if it's not night time or too foggy!

Accessing health services when you are away from home can be difficult. So health services in central Lakeland have created a website (www. lakedistricthealth.com) to guide visitors as to where to best access services.

# CHAPTER 6

# Farming

As a visitor, you will look up at the green fellsides, dotted with sheep, laced with stone walls. You may walk the fells, passing through the gates and over the stiles. But you will rarely meet a farmer. They are Lakeland's secretive custodians. Their work keeps the landscape looking as you expect it to look.

There are four farms in the Ambleside/Rydal area, if you include Skelwith Fold. They are all classified as hill farms and are all about sheep and a few cattle, because crops don't grow well on the poor stony acidic soil hereabouts. There is a wartime story about when local farmers were ordered to grow crops. Along came the Ministry inspector at the beginning of winter and asked the farmer how much wheat he had harvested that summer. "Don't know", said the farmer "it's not ripe yet."

Farming is not a job, it's a way of life. There are few days off, few late nights out. You won't meet farmers in the pub often, and seldom meet them anywhere away from their farms.

# THE CYCLE OF SHEEP FARMING

**SEPTEMBER**
FELL IS GATHERED EWES DISINFECTED FOR TICS AND LICE

**OCTOBER**
BREEDING CYCLE BEGINS

EWES BROUGHT OFF FELLS INTO LOWER PASTURES FOR TUPPING

MALE LAMBS TAKEN FOR SLAUGHTER FEMALES KEPT

MID JULY SHEEP GATHERED FROM FELLS AND SORTED. LAMBS SEPARATED FROM MOTHERS TO WEAN THEM. EWES CLIPPED, SHEARED AND RETURNED TO FELLS WITHOUT LAMBS

EVERY DAY TUPS HAVE 'RADDLE' PAINTED ON THEIR CHESTS – THIS CHANGES EVERY TWO WEEKS SO FARMERS CAN SEE IF THE TUP IS STILL WORKING

UNLESS YOUR DOG IS TRAINED NOT TO CHASE SHEEP, IT IS WISE TO KEEP THEM ON A LEAD AS SHEEP ARE NOT ALWAYS VISIBLE UNTIL IT IS TOO LATE. IF YOUR DOG IS CAUGHT CHASING SHEEP IT MAY BE SHOT.

END OF MAY RETURN TO FELL LAMBS REMAIN WITH MOTHER BECOMING 'HEFTED' TO THE FELL

AFTER TUPPING EWES ARE BROUGHT TO LOWER PARTS OF FELL. THEY ARE FED HAY, SILAGE AND FEED

LAMBING SHEEP CHECKED MULTIPLE TIMES A DAY- MALE LAMBS DESTINED FOR THE TABLE HAVE ELASTIC BANDS PUT ROUND TESTICLES SO THEY DROP OFF.

TWO WEEKS BEFORE LAMBS ARE DUE, EWES BROUGHT BACK DOWN TO LOWER PASTURES.

Rydal Farm is the largest locally and its land encompasses all that contained within the Fairfield Horseshoe and the meadowland between the A591 and the River Rothay. It has a fine 17<sup>th</sup> century barn, still in sound condition and in daily use. They have 1500 sheep. The farmer's year starts in autumn when the tups (rams) get their wicked way with dozens of ewes, which have been brought down to the valley bottoms, one tup to fifty ewes being a typical work load. This is timed to ensure that lambs are born in late April in this area, when the grass is growing, gestation being 150 days. Some lambs, known as North of England mule lambs, are bred from Swaledale ewes crossed with Blue faced Leicester rams. These are sold to southern farmers for fattening and turning into roasts, hotpots and shanks. Other lambs are bred from the native Herdwicks and Swaledales to maintain the flock. After lambing, the ewes are returned to the fell until clipping time in July and August. It costs more nowadays to clip a Lakeland ewe than the fleece is worth, but they have to be clipped. In September lambs are weaned from their mothers. Herdwick, the

Rough Fell and their close neighbour the Swaledale are the main breeds in this area. Herdwicks are famous because they don't need fencing in – they are 'hefted', which means they stay put on the land (the heaf) where they were weaned. They are also tasty to eat and their meat fetches good prices. Herdwick lambs are born black. After a year they lighten to a dark brown colour, then after their first shearing, the fleece lightens further to grey.

The fleece is coarse and well suited to use for carpet making. It is also a natural insulator and a new use for it is as loft insulation. The meat has a very distinct taste and was eaten at Queen Elizabeth II's 1953 coronation banquet.

"If they and their shepherds go, that is the end of the Lakeland where I have climbed, walked, skied and skated for nearly 80 years the Lakeland I have written about nearly all my life."
A Harry Griffin.

It is fair to say that hill farmers are discontented. They are also a bit bewildered as to what their present

# OVINE LOCALS

HERDWICK

SWALEDALE

BLUE LEICESTER

ROUGH FELL

day role is. They can't survive without subsidies, they are over regulated, at the mercy of the elements and under attack from environmentalists who want to rewild the fellsides. At the same time their sheep by grazing the fells preserve the look of the Lakeland landscape as most people wish to see it. Why do they carry on? It's a way of life they were probably born to and which they love... and if they don't carry on, the Lake District landscape will quickly revert to scrubland. So the sheep's main value now is said by cynics to be as a lawnmower.

Farmers also have significant issues with unthinking tourists. Particularly irritating are gates not closed, dogs let off leads among sheep, litter and climbing over drystone walls, dislodging the capstones, which results eventually in collapse of the wall. Farmers also have problems with the local wildlife, especially with badgers and foxes. Badgers are far more predatory than is popularly imagined. They will take new born lambs, although foxes usually get the blame. Farmers blame badgers also for the declining populations of hedgehogs and ground nesting birds and mostly disagree with the protected status badgers enjoy.

Another nuisance to the farmer locally is the Canada goose. Now breeding in what many think are excessive numbers, they eat valuable grazing on lake side meadows and create mess. One local farmer says going in Rydal Water is like swimming in goose poo.

They are also blamed by some for the decline of other wild fowl on Windermere.

Despite tourist provocation, most farmers do not aggressively confront people who wander off footpaths or otherwise roam uninvited on their land, provided they are not being a nuisance. The farmer will most likely ask if they are lost or need help. But if you need to enter farmland off designated rights of way, you should ask permission – the problem may be finding the farmer.

# CHAPTER 7

## A few famous dead residents

(There are many other locally famous
people but none are dead yet.)

### John Kelsick (1699-1723)

No school existed in Ambleside prior to 1723. In that
year a wealthy young man named John Kelsick died. He
was only twenty three. His fortune had been inherited
from his father George who appeared in Ambleside
in the mid-seventeenth century and who had shipping

Old Kelsick Hall

interests at the port of Whitehaven, owned property in Yorkshire and was a provisions merchant in Ambleside, based in this hall in what is now Church Street, shown in an engraving by William Green in 1808.

Parts of the hall still exist, though it is barely recognisable. It is divided now into shops and a café, but the original round chimney stacks are still in place. Above the house the picture shows the Royal Oak public house.

In his will John Kelsick left money and property in trust, the income from which was to be used to found a school in Ambleside and pay for its upkeep and staffing. In the manner of the time, this school was to be for boys only. In 1907 the Kelsick Foundation built a Grammar School, which later became part of the state system and was in use until 1965 when its function was assumed by the new comprehensive, The Lakes School. The Kelsick Educational Foundation still thrives and has been carefully administered over the centuries, continuing to assist young Ambleside boys and girls educationally, supporting some 'extras' not available in the state school system, and helping with higher education expenses, apprenticeships and youth activities.

Though little known elsewhere, for local people John Kelsick is probably the most famous name from the past. His remains lie in the old churchyard of St. Anne's.

## William Green (1760-1823)

William Green was an 'offcomer' who confessed to never really feeling accepted locally, even though his art did more than most to popularise Ambleside and benefit the town economically. Born in Manchester, he worked as a surveyor before arriving in Ambleside in 1800 determined to live as an artist. He lived in a house where Tesco is today in the Market Place and had a family of ten children to support by exhibiting and selling his prints at various locations. These prints were the earliest images to represent Ambleside as it really looked at the time and have thus become invaluable as historic records. Unsympathetic to conventional exaggerated depictions of the Lake District as a place of 'horrific' or 'terrifying' chasms and precipices, his etchings of the towns and landscapes drew on his feel for the real shape of the fells, the woods and the charm of the vernacular architecture and because he lived here, he saw the area in all its seasonal moods and lighting.

## William Wordsworth (1770-1850) and the "Lake Poets"

Wordsworth's heritage has been thoroughly appropriated by Grasmere even though he lived at Rydal far longer than he did at Dove Cottage and he also worked in Ambleside. He was, at one time, Distributor of Stamps for Westmorland, from an office in what has become known as the Stamp House in Church Street (now a restaurant). In 1820 he published his 'Guide through the District of the Lakes'. In 1842 he became the Poet Laureate, and resigned his office as Stamp Distributor.

The Lake Poets' main figures were William Wordsworth himself, Samuel Taylor Coleridge, and Robert Southey.

They were associated with several other poets and writers, including Dorothy Wordsworth, Charles Lamb, Hartley Coleridge, and Thomas De Quincey.

THOMAS DE QUINCEY

Ironically the popularity of the works of these poets encouraged readers to visit the Lakes, thus helping to destroy, as Wordsworth would have it, the isolation which made the area special. (Here we have the seeds of the perennial conundrum – does commercial development in the Lake District encourage too many visitors than is good for its preservation – or is more commercial development necessary to cater for the increasing numbers the National Park attracts?)

Wordsworth enjoyed the spectacle of Ambleside's annual rushbearing procession and it is said that he proposed that the route should be extended to Rydal Mount where he lived – it wasn't, but this may have been said in jest. His other contribution was to successfully campaign against the extension of the railway from Windermere to Ambleside, which with the hindsight of today was a pity – we could have had steam locos puffing around and retired second home owners keeping fit as firemen.

Coleridge wrote his best known poem, the Rime of the Ancient Mariner, in the Lakes although he didn't stay here for long. Thomas de Quincey lived at Dove Cottage in Grasmere, Fox Ghyll, Underloughrigg and later at Nab Cottage, Rydal, but seemed to have had little to do with Ambleside. He wasn't a happy man, suffering from birth with extreme bouts of neuralgia which probably caused his excessive use of opium and his rather unpleasant treatment of his friends. He edited the local paper, Westmorland Gazette, which was more right wing in those days and would have chimed with both Coleridge's and his social and political views. De Quincey made his name with the publication of "Confessions of an English Opium Eater", a book which he was well qualified to write. The Gazette sacked him after only a year, his addiction making him unreliable.

## Harriet Martineau (1802-1876)

North of the town centre on Rydal Road is an old Wesleyan chapel, long since converted to other uses. Behind and above this chapel is the private house called The Knoll. It was built on a knoll by Harriet Martineau in 1847. Miss Martineau had arrived from London and like a lot of newly arrived people in the area since, she began to make waves, much to the annoyance of the local establishment. An ardent social reformer, she was appalled at the living conditions of the local peasantry, as the working population were then called (and still are by some benighted offcomers), but as this was her first real taste of country life she may not have realised that such conditions were the norm throughout rural England.

She ranted against the insanitary and squalid homes, the irregular wages, drunkenness and wild behaviour of local people but she nevertheless admired their strength and endurance, their practical skills and willingness to learn.

Her reputation as a reforming journalist attracted widespread admiration from the liberal minded intelligentsia with the result that the Knoll was visited by a variety of the great and good, including Wordsworth, Coleridge, George Eliot, Nathaniel Hawthorne and the Bronte sisters.

Harriet was indeed a remarkable woman but her rejection of religion in a time when that was not acceptable probably contributed to the comparable and undeserved obscurity into which her legacy sank. Her interests embraced wildlife, botany, farming, feminism, anti-slavery, philosophy, politics and a passionate concern for the common good and for the working people of Ambleside, even setting up a local building society.

She was ahead of her time too in other ways – she enjoyed taking her bath in her garden. It is only now that among the more affluent residents of Ambleside outdoor hot tubs have become desirable.

From Ambleside Oral Archive – interviewee Joan Fitch born 1911, interviewed 1988:

> The Knoll is a very pleasant house and an historic one of course. It was built by Harriet Martineau. Wordsworth himself placed and planted one of the conifers in the garden, and came to call on her, and advised her not to be too lavish with hospitality though she would have many people calling upon her, and she would be wise to do as he did and

dispense a cup of tea or so, but charge extra for food. Wordsworth at his worst I'm afraid. But he was very friendly to her. It was in his parsimonious old age when he lived at Rydal Mount.

## From Ambleside Oral Archive - interviewee Barbara Dodd, born 1933, interviewed 2006:

[Harriett] decided that she would devote herself to the people here, but it wasn't just that, she became a leader writer for The Daily News which was a very important newspaper of the time, which was rather, I suppose, as the Independent, it was a radical newspaper would be nowadays. And she used to write sometimes as many as eight leaders a week, from Ambleside, and they would be published in London the next day. And when you think of all our emails and our telephones, but their communication system was wonderful.

By train?

It went down by train, yes. And apparently, in London at that time, there were twelve postal deliveries a day. Yes, twelve! So she would get The Times, in fact she persuaded Roland Hill - who you know was the 'Penny Post' man – who was a friend of hers in London, in the old days, to see that there was an extra delivery of post to Ambleside so that she could receive The Times every day, quickly go through it, decide what article she was going to write for The Daily News and off it would go the next morning, and published that same evening

## Charlotte Mason (1842-1923)

Charlotte Mason is famous in Ambleside as the founder of the college which bore her name. She became noted for her development of revolutionary methods of teaching children, believing that they should learn by contact with the best in art, literature and music from an early age. She co-founded the **Parents' Educational Union** (later **Parents' National Educational Union** – PNEU), an organisation that provided resources for the home education of children. Her methods are still widely followed in the USA.

In 1881 she founded the House of Education in Ambleside at Scale How, which became the Charlotte Mason college, later a teacher training college.

**From Ambleside Oral Archive – Percy Middleton born 1904, interviewed 1981:**

Were you there when Charlotte Mason died?

Oh yes, I was there then which was 1924(?)

Did she die at the college?

Yes, she died at the college.

What was the feeling of people when that happened throughout the village?

Well I should think they were really sorry because she was a nice and well-liked lady.

The village people knew her as well?

Yes, because she went off for a drive every day like, perhaps Grasmere or up by Tarn Hows or round there, but each day if it was anything like decent weather she went out for a ride in the carriage.

What was the carriage like?

Well it was what you would call a Victoria: you know a single horse carriage with a hood that you could pull up and of course you had a rug to go round and a brass foot warmer that you could fill with hot water to keep her feet warm.

Someone would drive her?

Yes she had a coachman to drive her.

And did he have a uniform on?

Yes, he had a top hat you know and … coat and when he came back, when he brought her back, we had the harness to, all the harness had to be sponged you know especially the insides where the horse had been sweating, so that it didn't make it sore. And the carriage: it had to be hosepiped down and washed and sponged and finished off with a wash leather.

Every day?

Every day, yes we did. Oh yes they looked after them well you know, because they were beautiful things you know, and highly varnished and you know they had to be kept up in high condition.

Do you know what happened to that carriage?

Yes: the coachman and I often used to, after Miss Mason had died and the funeral was over and about a week or two after everything had got settled, the coachman and I took this carriage to Windermere Station, and it went across to Ireland to a friend of Miss Mason's who I think was called Mrs Franklin: and after I took the horse out of the carriage. I rode him back to Ambleside and I think the coachman came back on the bus.

# Miss Armitt (1851-1911), Woodrow Wilson and Fred Yates

Born in 1854, Yates was already well known as a painter when he was invited to Ambleside to paint a now famous portrait of Charlotte Mason. He liked the Lake District and decided to bring up his daughter Mary here, living at Cote How in Rydal. It was there that he met and befriended Woodrow Wilson, the future US president, who rented a holiday house nearby (Loughrigg Cottage). At Wilson's inauguration as President, Yates was invited to Washington to paint his portrait. Wilson presented Yates with the flag on which he rested his hand while taking the oath of office.

Mary Louisa Armitt (1851-1911) was a teacher, writer, ornithologist and philanthropist. The Armitt sisters lived at Rydal, in Manor Cottage, the first cottage on the left after Pelter Bridge, going north. Mary wrote an amazingly detailed history of Rydal. She is famous locally for founding the Armitt Library, now the Armitt Library and Museum which you should visit while you're here.

Canon H D Rawnsley wrote this sonnet in praise of Mary Louisa and her sister:

"As in some inland solitude a shell
Still gently murmurs of its home, the deep,
So in the world of being beyond all sleep
Where those two happy sister spirits dwell,
This book-lined room, this simple Students' cell
Shall, in the silence, pure memorial keep
Of those who sowed that other minds might reap
Their wisdom won from lake and wood and fell;
And as we gather up their gentle lore,
Made rich by jewels from their treasury,
The whispers grow " Behold ! These souls had power
Because with patient heart and loving eye
They learned that man and bird and beast and flower
Were in God's purpose friends for evermore."

Miss Armitt used to come up to Hart Head and ask my father about this, that and the other when she was doing the book you see. Do you remember her clearly? Oh yes, we used to go there once a week or once a fortnight, we had to go there, she lived in that very nice house with the lattice windows, first one you come to where the reading room is, I don't know whether it was once a week or once a fortnight for sewing lessons and make – she used to save cardboard boxes and she used to cut them out to make them into beds, little beds for to put dolls in for Christmas. She was nice, was Miss Armitt, there were two of them really, and then there was a Mrs Harris, a sister. She was fond of children? Did she run these classes on her own? Oh yes. She'd got two maids. All those houses in Rydal had maids then. Was she a very educated sort of person? Was she very learned? Oh yes, she was. What sort of things did she want to come and ask your father, all local things? All about the sheep and different things you know, as she was making up the book. And then she'd go up to Miss Yates who lived in one of the cottages up above Hart Head, you'd remember Miss Yates, quite a big person, she used to go to Scale How, she used to walk along with me in the morning when I was coming to school, she went up to Scale How. She worked at Charlotte Mason? No, she was a pupil. Well no, I mustn't say that. Her father was an artist you know, Mr Yates the artist and you know they weren't too well off and she got her education by teaching some of the younger children and President Woodrow Wilson from America, he came and took one of those houses under Loughrigg by the Stepping Stones one summer, and he used to come walking past our place to Mr Yates' the artist to look at his paintings and he bought a few and he commissioned Mr Yates to go out to America and paint him in his robes, which he did do. I've still got the card of Niagara Falls which he sent to me when he was there. Was that whilst he was President? Yes, he took Loughrigg Holme I think it was, this side of the Stepping Stones, he took it for six months. Oh you forget lots of things.

# Alfred Heaton Cooper (1863-1929)

Alfred Heaton Cooper, landscape artist, came to the Lakes in 1890 from Bolton and after trying his luck in Coniston he decided correctly that there were more tourists in Ambleside likely to buy his work. From Norway, where he had lived and married, he imported in kit form a log cabin as a studio – see 'Notable Buildings' later. Alfred made his name by illustrating the early tourist guide books published by A. & C. Black, using colour plates. He was an accomplished watercolourist and his paintings fetch good prices. After Alfred's death in 1929 his son, the better known painter William Heaton Cooper, moved to Grasmere and built the Heaton Cooper Studio which is still owned and run by his descendants. But it nearly didn't happen – see below.

From Ambleside Oral Archive, interviewee Alison Carrington-Smith, born 1909, interviewed 1991:

> ...we used to go and visit Alfred Heaton Cooper's studio which is on Lake Road, and we used to go in and we were only about 10 and 12 I think. And he was the kindest man you can imagine. He had

a bright red bow-tie, and a big moustache, and he was always very busy, and he was painting, and we used to go in and waste hours of his time looking at his pictures and he'd drop everything and he'd come round with us and he'd take the trouble to explain where they were, and how he'd painted them, and asked us which one we liked. And we didn't only do this just occasionally, we did it regularly. And he was never anything but very kind.

...that was the Ambleside/Waterhead Carnival, which was about 1924 somewhere like that. I think they had one every year. And it was always very cold you know, and it was rather new to be towed behind a motor boat in those days. Of course it's nothing like they do now, but – holding on to ropes – you know. Well Heaton Cooper the young son of the artist – Alfred Heaton Cooper – he wanted to try and he was very plucky really. It was a very cold day, and he was going along quite well, and then he fell off, and nobody took much notice 'cos they thought he'd come up again: and he came sort of half up, and then went down again. And my brother who was in the boat, in the motor boat, was towing him, realised what was happening, and went straight over with his hat on and his shoes, and mackintosh and everything, and he had to find Heaton who was very nearly drowned. And he brought him up, and he'd got cramp, and he would have drowned definitely, if Norman hadn't got there at once.

## Kurt Schwitters (1887–1947)

Another erstwhile resident was the avant-garde artist Kurt Schwitters, who lived briefly in the town immediately after WW2. There's a plaque on the house in Millans Park where he spent his last days. Schwitters was a German who fell foul of the Nazis, his abstract work being condemned as degenerate. He fled to Norway, only to have the Germans annex that country. So he came to England and after internment in the Isle of Man as an enemy alien he ended up here, in poverty, after a stay in London, where he met Edith Thomas. They moved to Ambleside in 1945. Local people, who mostly completely failed to understand, somewhat understandably, 'what his art was about' were kind and gave him portrait commissions, or accepted drawings in local cafés in return for food.

Although Schwitters is regarded now as one of the fathers of modern art, his work is not widely appreciated or understood, although it is now of great value. Ambleside's Armitt Museum has a collection of works, mainly of the more conventional paintings he did while here as he struggled to make a living, and some of his abstract works. His last great unfinished collage, created from found objects, the Merzbau, was created at Elterwater and is now in Newcastle's Hatton Gallery. (We want it back.)

Schwitters was buried in Ambleside but his remains were exhumed in 1970 and taken by his family to Hanover, his home town. There is a memorial stone at the site of his grave in Ambleside parish churchyard.

## From Ambleside Oral Archive – interviewee Valmai Varty, born 1921, interviewed 1998

Well, first of all I saw him – it would be sort of early August or late July 1946 and he was quite a large figure. He gave you the opinion of being a large ..... I don't know whether he was tall but in his body, he wasn't a lean, spare sort of man, he had quite a lot of flesh on him actually but he was clothed in a black beret and a black raincoat, like a Burberry raincoat, that sort of thing and he looked rather menacing, this figure dressed all in black but that's the first time and the last time I ever saw him. Well, he seemed to be very generous with my in-laws because there was a portrait of her, there was a portrait of her husband and the most wonderful painting of roses I've ever seen. It was framed about 9 x 9 inches, something like that and that was a wide frame about an inch and a half wide and so the picture was just a little one, a little square in the middle but you could have picked those roses – it seemed as though you could have picked them. And then he made a collage on a postcard which I think these days would have brought in tens of thousands of pounds and it was the most horrible thing I've ever seen. For one thing, it had a bus ticket stuck on it and it had a sticky toffee paper on it and in the middle was the front of a Players Please packet of cigarettes. But somebody bought them, somebody bought that off her – I wonder how much somebody's paying for it now – and it was a Frenchman. There was another portrait of a woman in Grasmere, Mrs. Horner of Horner's Toffees fame. Now he painted her and when she received it, she didn't like it. She commissioned him to do this for her you see, so she wouldn't pay for it and he took it back or his lady friend took it back. Now when Schwitters died two years after I met him – he died '48 I think – when she realised that there was so much fuss made about Schwitters, she tried all sorts of ways to get her picture back and they wouldn't let her have it back, so …. She's in Devon I think – well, she's dead now anyway. I suppose during the war the Ambleside people were very generous to accept a German refugee, Kurt Schwitters, in their midst and your parents-in-law particularly, in helping him and looking after him.

Well, I don't know how generous they would be really, because everything was rationed and it was all Hitler's fault, you know, that's why he escaped Germany of course. First to Norway and then when the Germans came to Norway, he was very lucky to be able to escape again. So he had two chances whereas lots of our soldiers didn't have one, did they? And it must have been very difficult for your husband, coming back from the war and finding a German... Well, he was very jealous actually of the fact that my in-laws made such a fuss of him because as he says, he's been fighting Germans for eight years and then he comes home and finds one sitting down, having a cup of tea in the house!

# CHAPTER 8

## Notable buildings and places

(Inclusion here does not indicate that all premises are open to the public)

### St Mary's Church

The parish church was completed in 1854 as the old chapel of St Anne's at How Head could no longer accommodate an increasing population combined with growing numbers of visitors. The architect was Sir George Gilbert Scott.

The church was commissioned at a time when the movers and shakers of Ambleside viewed with pride and satisfaction the growing popularity of the town as a holiday destination and the work coincided with the spectacular development of tourist accommodation in the streets in the lower town, as opposed to the old town north of Stock Beck.

So a grandiose building seemed appropriate, with a capacity designed for population growth and to reflect the new importance of the town. Perhaps with this in mind old George Scott decided to give the church a spire, quite out of character with Lake District churches which mostly find a tower quite adequate.

ST. MARYS PARISH CHURCH

This spire has subsequently proved to be rather an expensive liability. The first design was taller but it was found that the substructure would not support its weight, so the height was reduced. Instead of building it with local slate (durable and waterproof) it was decided for ease of working to use sandstone. Maintenance of the spire is now a constant concern. The sandstone cladding has proved porous and the ingress of large amounts of water seriously damaged the original organ, happily now restored. Attempts to repair the leakages have not been very successful and have been a drain on resources, to the extent that some people are suggesting that the spire should be demolished. So perhaps another local controversy will rear its head at some point.

St Mary's has a set of eight bells which are said to be the finest between Manchester and Glasgow. As a result they are popular with campanologists from away who enjoy ringing a full peal, which takes about three and a half hours. After local complaints, these peals are now restricted to about four per annum, in winter. If you like bells that's a shame. If you really don't like them, four is thought to be tolerable, but not by everyone. The local captain kindly gives advanced warning.

Inside the church is a mural created in 1944 on the back wall depicting a Rushbearing ceremony. It is by Gordon Ransom, one time lecturer at the Royal College of Art, which was evacuated to Ambleside during the second world war. The mural depicts 62 figures in four scenes, representing inhabitants of Ambleside at that time. However, their identities were deliberately obscured, with heads transposed on to different bodies. Gordon Ransom returned to Ambleside in the 1990s, but declined to name anyone in the mural. It is nevertheless a matter of some local pride to be identified as one of these figures. If you are still alive of course.

## St Anne's Chapel (as was)

At the top of Chapel Hill in old Ambleside stands the former St Anne's Chapel, now converted into apartments.

This hilltop site has possibly been a place of worship for far longer than history records. There is conjecture that

ST. ANNES CHAPEL

even pre-Christian settlers and Vikings may have used it for whatever they did to appease the gods that controlled the natural phenomena which they feared. But it was not until the 16th century that Ambleside folk erected a rudimentary chapel on the site. Prior to that they walked to Grasmere or Windermere to worship, depending on whether they lived north or south of Stock Beck, the boundary between the two parishes.

This little chapel gradually grew but local people still had to travel to Grasmere or Windermere to get christened, married or buried and as Ambleside's population grew, this became increasingly a cause of resentment. Eventually the chapel was in 1676 given the right hold its own christenings and funerals, much to the annoyance of the Grasmere and Bowness clerical incumbents who thereby lost tithes.

A curate was appointed, whose low income obliged him to teach boy pupils at one penny per day and who was given the right to take the pennies paid by local children to attend cockfights.

It is recorded by Mary Armitt in her article of 1905 Ambleside Town and Chapel that, after a year or so:

> "A period of decadence had, indeed, come over the ministers of the church, if not over the body of it. To the earnest religious feeling of the seventeenth century had succeeded a general carelessness of living, and a habit of using the endowments of the church for purely personal ends. The Rev. Jonathan Myles had not been above sitting in the ale-house with boon companions, where his extraordinary action one day in "bullocking the constable" entailed serious consequences, gave business to the Quarter Sessions, and set the whole town by the ears."

The church was rebuilt a couple of times as the local population and tourism increased, until in 1854 the grandiose new St Mary's Parish Church was built and St Anne's later became a community hall. Its little churchyard contains the grave of John Kelsick, mentioned previously.

## From Ambleside Oral Archive. interviewee Theo Stephenson, born 1917, interviewed 1984:

We'll go back and talk about St Anne's, the original Church. You say there was no graveyard around but did some burials take place? Burials took place under the floor, as was the custom. Now when they did some alterations at St Anne's just after the Second World War and they made it into a village community hall, they took up the old pews and took up the flag floor, and within a matter of 6–8 inches, 6–12 inches there were graves underneath it, and that's as far down as they went: so what date they stopped burying under the floor I haven't the faintest idea. There were no markings on the flags that were taken up as to when the burials had taken place or anything, or whether the Church as we know it today was built over the top of them, because it was rebuilt in 1812 you see. It might have been the original gravestones on the graveyard and then they built the Church on top. Yes but there's none of the gravestones, headstones in the churchyard dated, well I think the earliest date is about 1804, 1805 or something like that. Which suggests you might be right, that the church was built over some of the graves. What did they have to do when they discovered the graves? Well they... same as they're supposed to do, they're supposed to take them up and rebury them: do they? ...When they did this last lot of alterations, turning the place into living accommodation, they had to get the drainage in and they found an awful lot of bones again under the floor of the building and I know where they were dumped, they were just dumped in the basement of the boiler house and filled in.

So if you own one of the second homes in St Anne's, you are living above heaps of the bones of the ancestors of local people who were here long before you and will be long after you've gone.

## Methodist Church

The large church in Millans Park was built in 1898 when there was obviously a big enough congregation to justify it. Its adjoining hall became a useful venue for many local events. In 2007 with a dwindling attendance and coinciding with the fundraising for and construction of the new Parish Centre, the Methodists decided to convert their church and hall into shared ownership local occupancy housing and, in a partnership with the Anglicans, to move their mission into part of the Parish Centre. This was an admirable act of great social benefit to the community – conversion into expensive luxury apartments would have been the obvious option for anyone with less of a social conscience.

## Mater Amabilis Catholic Church and Wansfell Tower

After the Reformation, a Catholic presence in Ambleside was not apparent until 1878, when Mass was first celebrated in the Bonney family's home at Mill Cottage in Rydal Road (now called Idle Mill). Shortly after in 1892, the Catholic 'Tin Chapel' was erected on the site of the present church, which replaced it in the nineteen thirties. Close by, on the corner of Lake Road and Wansfell Road, stands Wansfell Tower. It is now apartments and was once a hotel but it was originally built in 1892 and intended to become a Catholic priory and prep school but funds ran out after a few years. An eroded inscription on a foundation stone records the year of construction.

## The Bridge House – the true story – probably

Images of this quaint and ancient little structure have become a symbol, dare we say a trade mark, of the town. Not many visitors neglect to take a photo of it, usually with their companions in shot. The main road through the town never used to follow its current route and the buildings opposite the Bridge House weren't there when it was built. That space was part of the garden of Ambleside Hall which went down to Stock Beck. The hall was quite small. In eighteenth century Ambleside any stone building bigger than a hovel was called a Hall. What's left of the Hall is now invisible from the road except for The Old House in Smithy

Brow and the Golden Rule pub, parts of the interiors of which were part of the Hall. Across the river, there was an orchard. The owners of the Hall, the Braithwaites, built the Bridge House in 1723. It was built as a bridge of course, which it isn't now, the south exit having been blocked up when the orchard and land beyond were sold.

The upper floor was used as an apple store for the produce of the orchard beyond, being cool and humid from the water below, thus ideal for the purpose.

By 1819 the Bridge House was a tourist attraction, being a tea room in the short summer season and a weaving house for the rest of the year. Then it was taken by Chairy Rigg, who somehow managed to have a workshop there making wicker baskets and repairing chairs and also accommodating his wife and six children. By the end of the 19th century it was being used by a shoemaker, who also kept his pigeons on the upper floor. Thus that old story is not a load of cobblers.

The building was 200 years old before it started to decay. Having become a tourist draw, it was bought and restored by the townspeople and presented in 1928 to the National Trust, to whom we now warily entrust its future, for in 2014 the Trust wanted to put steel railings beside the stairs, having been frightened by Health & Safety. Local cries of "Sacrilege!" and "Vandalism!" defeated the plans. So now if you fall off the stairs, don't blame the Trust.

For nearly 300 years this little house has withstood the ravages of time, tourism and floods, even the recent ones which have devastated so many other local bridges. Amazing! Happily there are still Braithwaites and Riggs in Ambleside and until very recently a chair maker and a cobbler.

THE MARKET HALL

## Market Hall

Dating from 1863 this listed picturesque Victorian Gothic building was originally the local Mechanics' Institute, founded to provide adult education for working men, especially in technical subjects, and it also acted as a reading room. The building has many interesting features – steep roofs, corner buttresses, arched windows and an octagonal louvre. A square 3-storeyed tower on south-east corner houses the town clock. The building is now one of several owned by a local welfare charity, the rents from which enable the trustees to offer help to local people in need.

## Rothay Park

This is a beautiful and much used facility with mature trees, rhododendrons, daffodils in spring, wide grassy expanses and a children's playground. Once marshland, it was drained by diversion of Stock Beck and donated to the Council by Colonel Rhodes in the late 19th century. During the two world wars it was partly cultivated as allotments. Beloved of dog walkers, footballers and picnickers, its central path leads from Vicarage Road to Under Loughrigg and forms the start of several popular walks.

# Log House

Alfred Heaton Cooper, born in 1863, was a painter from Bolton, determined to make a living selling landscape watercolours. He rightly figured that the best places to do this were beauty spots popular with

THE LOG HOUSE

affluent tourists, such as the Lake District. But first he tried the Norwegian fjord country, where he lived for 5 years and fell in love with and married a local girl. Needing better sales, he tried Southport and then Coniston, whither he imported from Trondheim a traditional Norwegian log house in kit form to use as a studio, probably as a gimmick but no doubt also to make his Norwegian wife feel less isolated. Sales weren't sufficient and he decided to move to Ambleside which attracted more visitors. The log house was dismantled and moved more than once, ending up eventually where it is now and was Alfred's base until his death in 1929. Currently a restaurant, externally it is little changed.

## The Fulling Mill and Idle Mill

The restaurant called the Fulling Mill actually is in an old fulling mill dating from the late Middle Ages. It was later converted into a large 3-storey woollen mill in 1795. It was run by the Cooper family and latterly the Partridges, then converted to a saw mill in the 1830s after which it fell into disuse. In 1999 the owner Adrian Sankey gathered local craftsmen to restore the dam, the mill race and the waterwheel, the internal belts and the gearing which now form an interesting backdrop to the extensive menu.

Adjoining the Fulling Mill is an extension of the woollen mill. It has had many uses since, being in living memory a private dwelling and a café known as Mill Cottage. When the penal laws against Catholics were finally removed, the property was owned by a Mr Bonney and the first legal Mass in Ambleside was celebrated there, as there was no Catholic church in the town. Now converted into self catering apartments, it has been wittily and appropriately renamed Idle Mill as it is not working and you can idle away your leisure time there.

## Stock Ghyll Bobbin Mill (now holiday apartments)

This large building, visible across Stock Beck from Stock Ghyll Lane, was once the home of a large bobbin factory, and also from the early 1900s a laundry servicing the accommodation industry, though it is now hardly recognizable as such. It was started about 1840 by the Horrax family and became Ambleside's major employer as the demand from the textile industry for wooden bobbins grew. The factory obtained its timber from local coppiced woodland and used a combination of steam and water power for wood turning. Waste wood from the turning process was used to fire the steam boilers in an early example of recycling. As in many factories at the time, working conditions were hard and accidents, including fires, occurred in cold candle lit workshops. After WW2 plastic moulding began to make wooden bobbins redundant so the business gradually wound down and closed.

## University of Cumbria Ambleside Campus

This complex of buildings developed from an original hall built in 1790, called Greenbank. It was the home of industrialist Benson Harrison who had an iron foundry in Ulverston and was a leading citizen of Ambleside. It was bought in 1891 by Charlotte Mason who founded her House of Education there, renaming the house Scale How. It became known as Charlotte Mason College,

UNIVERSITY OF CUMBRIA
AMBLESIDE CAMPUS

being first a school to train young women as governesses, who would educate children abroad during the days of Empire, then a teacher training establishment. After Miss Mason's death in 1923 the college was taken over by the Workers Education Association, then eventually the County Council. Until the mid sixties the college was for females only but then they nervously took three mature men as a start and, with great trepidation as to what damage they would do amongst the women students, gradually allowed 18 year old men. The Charlotte Mason name survived until due to politically inspired financial problems beyond the ken or control of local people it was taken over by Lancaster University which then managed to create a £9 million deficit, so it was then taken over by St Martin's College, Lancaster. Round about this time it began to lose its identity as Charlotte Mason College despite protests locally and by ex-students.

Anyway, the St Martin's arrangement was not successful and it came under the control of the newly created University of Cumbria who before long decided controversially to 'mothball' it. Mighty protests were launched by locals, some of whom thought that the day of judgment had arrived and we were all financially doomed without students' spending. Other sections of the community who had no financial interest were quite pleased to get student cars off the streets. Some second homes let to students were hastily converted to self-catering holiday lets. In fact although there were staff redundancies no businesses closed as a result and when after three years the University got its finances sorted out and decided to re-open the campus, the town was in two minds whether it wanted the students back.

The Lake District National Park Authority however decided that reopening the campus was a community asset and eased restrictions on change of use for some properties which the university wanted to dispose of, indeed the university made that a condition of re-opening the campus. So the LDNPA gave planning permission for a vast new cluster of student accommodation apartments in Rydal Road to "help relieve the pressure on local private houses". Controversy rages locally about why some redundant buildings were put on the market for developers to convert into hotels, instead of the University doing good by the locals and creating more affordable homes in them or turning them into student residences. The answer of course is that hotel developers will pay more, although no development proposals have yet succeeded. So the relationship between the town and the University has been somewhat strained and not just over that issue. Students' cars parked long term in residential streets are an ongoing problem. (So are tourists' cars.) However a more conciliatory attitude by the University to local concerns are improving relations.

## Riverside Lodge (previously Seven Gates)

This house by Rothay Bridge has suffered at least two name changes. Before becoming Seven Gates it was called simply The Cottage and was home in the 18th century to the prominent Benson Harrison family. It was also for a short time the home of Rev Frederick Faber (born 1814) who was famous first as a poet and then a composer of hymns. He was befriended by Wordsworth. His struggles with religious faith finally persuaded him to "go over to Rome". He became a Catholic priest and was instrumental in the founding of the Brompton Oratory. His hymn *Faith of our Fathers* is a Catholic favourite.

RIVERSIDE LODGE

From Ambleside Oral Archive - interviewee Joyce Cockcroft, interviewed 1984:

> ...but thereby hangs a story because during the days that Parson Daws was the parson at St. Anne's, Faber the poet came as his assistant for a short time and tutor to the Benson Harrison boys and Faber was very keen on music and so, as old Parson Daws

was failing, he took the services at St. Anne's and he formed a choir there amongst which were very prominent members of the Benson Harrison boys and apparently it was a great success, this choir and Canon Rawnsley, in one of his books, quotes that some old lady had said that before Faber came Ambleside was a very dark place, but he brought light into it when he created a choir at St. Anne's. And they also had evensong at St. Anne's which was never had before and this old lady said what a pity it was he went over to the other side because he eventually became a Roman Catholic.

## Rothay Manor

Built in 1835 for John Crosfield, a merchant from Liverpool, this house was originally known as Rothay Bank. The veranda and balcony, are unusual, being made of cast iron. The house came into the ownership of Sir George Mills McKay, a Warrington industrialist, treasurer of the English-Speaking Union and a Sheriff of London, in the early 20th century. The artist Alfred Heaton Cooper was a frequent visitor for evening soirees and card games. The house became a hotel in 1936 and had its name changed to

Rothay Manor. It was acquired by Mrs Bronwen Nixon in 1966, who over 20 years built its excellent reputation. Mrs Nixon was also instrumental in having a very welcome heavy lorry ban put on the A591 through the town. Sadly she was murdered in her bedroom in 1986 by a disgruntled former employee. The hotel continued until 2016 to be operated by her sons, Nigel and Stephen Nixon. As from 2016 it is under new ownership.

## Fox How and Fox Ghyll (private)

FOX GHYLL

Fox How, a large house Underloughrigg, built in 1833, was a venue for the intelligentsia and literati in the 19th century. It was built for Dr Arnold, headmaster of Rugby School and later lived in by his poet son Matthew.

Just down the hill from Fox How, the unspoilt Victorian residence called Fox Ghyll, named for the adjacent beck, offers bed and breakfast. It was from 1821 to 1825 the home of Thomas de Quincey. A Mr & Mrs Forster also lived there, he being MP for the borough of Bradford, and the first Minister of Education, she being Matthew Arnold's daughter. So the Arnold clan must have liked this quiet but often gloomy north facing corner of Underloughrigg. Visitors to both houses included all the Lake poets and literati, Harriett Martineau, Charlotte Brontë and no doubt other visiting intelligentsia for whom the poets had turned the Lake District into one of the English alternative destinations to the Grand Tour of Europe which, as mentioned before, Napoleon had temporarily rendered a no-go area.

From Ambleside Oral Archive - interviewee Joyce Cockcroft, interviewed 1984:

   ...and Charlotte Brontë visited the Arnolds who lived at Fox How, and Dr. Arnold built Fox How and Wordsworth was instrumental in keeping his eye on the building project while Dr. Arnold was at Rugby School and he used to come over and supervise the gardens when they were being laid out. And when Dr. Arnold died his family came to live there permanently and his daughter lived across the road at Fox Ghyll and she married a man called Forster – wasn't he Foreign Secretary? He was a great reformer anyway. And there's a plaque in Rydal Church commemorating the last of the Arnold sisters who died either in the early 30s or late 20s, from Fox How. Then my recollection of Fox How after that it was in my day it was bought by Bishop Bulley when he became Bishop of Penrith after having quitted Ambleside as Vicar and he lived there. And then he sold it.

## From Ambleside Oral Archive, interviewee Alice Blezzard born 1880, interviewed 1978:

Well these children were all rather articulate because they've lived in this district where the great poets lived, they were household names to them, Wordsworth, Coleridge, the other man, Southey and then Mrs. Felicia Hemans lived at Dove Nest and she wrote The Better Land which was a very popular song in our young days. 'I hear you speak of a better land' do you not know it? What was her name again? Felicia Hemans, and the children knew some of the present writers personally, Gordon Wordsworth you see, the grandson of William lived Under Loughrigg, so did Matthew Arnold and Sir Edwin Arnold, they lived Under Loughrigg and we would meet them and they would be coming into the town. Now there were no libraries as such here in those days except you could borrow a novel or two from the one or two book shops in Ambleside but if you wanted a book on some subject, a more abstruse subject you could ask at the Council offices, we had our own Council in those days, and they would get it for you from Kendal.

## Nab Cottage

Alongside the A591 at Rydal, this ancient 16th century dwelling is nowadays home to a residential English Language school as well as offering bed & breakfast. In a previous age it was a farmstead including the surrounding fields but now stands alone. Famous in the early 19th century as the home of Thomas de Quincey, journalist and opium addict, its later tenant was the witty raconteur Hartley Coleridge, son of poet Samuel.

## Dove Nest (now The Samling)

Built in about 1780, the house was originally owned by the same person who owned Dove Cottage in Grasmere, so Wordsworth used to walk across the fells to Dove Nest to pay his rent. He and his sister Dorothy had picnics in the grounds and he wrote a sonnet about it. Later, it was lived in by Victorian poet Felicia Hemans – forgotten now except for a poem, *The Boy Stood On The Burning Deck*, much bowdlerised by schoolboys and rugby players.

The Samling is now a luxury hotel which has played host to many A-list celebrities.

## Galava Roman Fort

Hardly a building, more a ruin, the remains of this fort at Waterhead are somewhat sad. It is pleasant to wander among them and imagine the goings-on here nearly two thousand years ago when it was a thriving military base, part of the Romans' attempt to pacify the unruly and rebellious tribes of northern Britannia. Then the fort had high walls and entrance gates, the stones long since plundered to help build modern Ambleside. To the north of the fort there was a settlement extending at least to where the Rothay Manor hotel is now. There is a Roman well in the hotel's cellar. Galava field is owned by the National Trust. English Heritage have erected some interpretative signs. Their wish to develop the site into a more informative "visitor experience" is on hold since the field is let long term for grazing land. Beware cows with calves if you bring your dog. A feature of the field is the large well maintained traditional two storey barn with an inscription *Miss J. Jackson 1831*.

## Kelsick Cottages, Kirkstone Road

This building was the first home of the Kelsick School, funded in his will by John Kelsick. The school subsequently moved to Vicarage Road, where it is now a children's day nursery. The original school became small cottages, some of which have now found a new role as holiday lets. It's fair to say it was more use to local people then than it is today.

# Eller How, Ellerigg Road

In 1852 Anne Jemima Clough, from Liverpool, opened a school here for the children of local farmers and trades people. The school thrived, soon employing three teachers. Pupils included young children up to ten years and then girls, who were not eligible to attend the Kelsick School. Miss Clough apparently took a

ELLER HOW FOLLY

personal interest in each of them, and was evidently regarded as much as a friend as a teacher. Keen to promote the education of women, she went on to become a respected educationalist and principal of Newnham College, Cambridge.

Eller How was later the home of the Boyles, retired diplomats. In the grounds they built a stone tower, best viewed from the track up to High Sweden bridge. It was built to resemble a ruin and their house guests were invited to add a stone with their names on.

Around 1910 they also kept two young crocodiles in a large temperature controlled pond in the grounds. According to local lore, one day the heating went out of control and the crocs were 'boyled' to death. Mr Harry Boyle used to feed red squirrels – they took nuts from his hand.

## Ellerbeck, Ellerigg Road

This house was the home of John Lund (1912–2014). He was a microbial ecologist whose methods were emulated by three generations of scientists. After distinguished academic achievements in zoology and botany, in 1944 he joined the staff of the Freshwater Biological Association as an algologist. He began his work on the ecology of planktonic algae of the English Lake District, initially at Wray Castle and then from 1950, at the Ferry House, Windermere.

John was elected as a Fellow of the Royal Society in 1963, awarded a CBE in 1965 and was President of the British Phycological Society. He was an expert in the analysis and causes of toxic blue-green algae in Windermere.

In an interview in 2012 for Ambleside Oral Archive, John had this to say in answer to a question about the future of the planet:

> So do you think, none of us can really predict the future, but do you think that science will help limit environmental damage or will it just go on as the population goes up and we become increasingly consumers?
>
> *Certainly it should help to limit it but the real problem is population and if we go on multiplying, I*

am sorry but I don't believe that we can really do very much because when it comes down to brass tacks human beings have got to be fed and if they are fed then they breed. You see nobody believes in Malthus nowadays, because Malthus said donkeys years ago that we should all be starving. What he didn't realise was that science would put off the evil day and it has put it off right up to now. But you can't put it off forever chum, anybody who's ever grown a culture or anything knows that perfectly well, there's a limit and how much longer we can go on is not for me to say. I don't pretend to be a specialist on these matters, all I know is you can't go on increasing the population for ever and ever because the resources that that population needs are not everlasting and ever increasing.

John Lund died at home in Ambleside, aged 102.

# Ambleside Park, Waterhead

This former mansion, which is now a private holiday hotel for staff of the John Lewis Partnership, was built by the MacIvers, the shipping family who first had their own liners and then became founding partners in the Cunard Line. The house was called Wanlass How. The grounds of the house originally extended to the lake shore with a pier for the family boats. When the new Borrans Road was to be built between the house and the lake, the family gave the land which now forms Borrans Park to the local authority, thus giving public access to the lake shore in a fine philanthropic gesture. They also built a handsome shelter by the shore, which still stands. At the same time a new lawn was made, to be level with the house and supported on stone built barrel vaults, the ends of which are visible from the road as part of the retaining wall. When the MacIvers left, the house was bought by the Liverpool Orphanage and they had 74 orphans there. It was used during WW2 to house evacuees from Liverpool, then used as an innovative knitting factory, whose claim to fame was the invention of the tartan poncho, supplied to Marks & Spencer, which became a famous fashion symbol of the 1960s.

In the 1970s the house was a venue for local dances and events before being bought by John Lewis. It is not open to the public.

In those days it was very expensive to bring stone
in so the lawn was all built arched over a series of
caves, so the lawn actually was hollow and it used to
be quite an excitement to go through the caves with
candles and a piece of string that you unreeled from
the grating in case you got lost. There were a series
of walls that supported it, some of them went up to
the roof and had like a sheep-hole underneath that
you crawled through: some of the walls only went
half-way and they had a sort of stile in them – I
suppose there must have been about a dozen or more
rooms down there, under the lawn. Could you stand
up in them? Oh yes, yes and it had stalactites and
stalagmites and don't let anybody ever tell you that
stalactites take thousands of years to grow because
these have only been there for a hundred years. Are
these caves still there?. No. Unfortunately, after
the John Lewis Partnership acquired Wanlass How,
they were going to use that way to bring gas in and
they discovered that they were going to collapse. In
fact they had been wondering what the hole was in

one of the flower beds – they thought it was just a rabbit hole. Then somebody dropped a stone, heard it going down a long way, so they broke them open and had them filled in.

## The Stepping Stones, Under Loughrigg

The stepping stones have been there for a very long time, but no one knows exactly how long. However, it is now thought that the present set of stones replaced an earlier and probably more precarious crossing. The present set date from around 1800 and were built for the convenience of his family and servants by Thomas Fleming who owned the house above, now called Stepping Stones but then known as Cockstone. Thomas, who lived from 1763 –1840, was related to the Le Flemings of Rydal Hall.

## Broadlands (as was)

This large house in Borrans Road is now known, inexplicably, as Borrans Park, which it isn't, and has suffered the fate of many larger homes. In recent memory it was the regional office of the

National Trust, then it became the Borrans Hotel. Now it is divided into second or holiday homes. Borrans is actually a local word not found in dictionaries, meaning piles of boulders, probably. In its time as the house of gentry, it was the home of Mrs Claude and her daughters, a lady known, according to Harriet Martineau, for hospitality and "care of the sick, the ignorant, and orphans". How times change!

# CHAPTER 9

# Traditions, Sports and Pastimes

Ambleside as a community has always been interested in its past. For instance, memories of what shops used to be where before mass tourism changed everything, or ruined it, according to your point of view, are a recurrent theme. Older locals will tell you about how such and such a useless coffee shop, outdoor clothing shop or restaurant used to be a useful butcher, draper, baker, grocer, tailor or bank. This of course has its roots in a quiet resentment about how nowadays 'it's all for the tourists', which of course it mostly is. If you own a hotel, guest house or cafe, there are not enough tourists. If you are retired, or a farmer, or a street cleaner, there are too many. In a way these opposing views result in a kind of uneasy balance, enabling the town to retain its identity as a community rather than letting it degenerate entirely into a soulless marketable resort facility. In spite of this there are some visitors and some business men who think that's exactly what it should be and that we should willingly prostitute our identity in whatever way is necessary to provide them with a 'good visitor experience'. After all, they've been condescending enough to bestow a little of their 'hard earned' affluence on us so why shouldn't we give them the grateful servitude that they crave?

## Felony

There was a time when isolated rural communities had no police force. In those days a lot of poor people did a lot of poaching and thieving in order to feed their families. This didn't suit those who owned the stuff they stole and in order to get these miscreants hanged or transported to penal servitude in Tasmania, Associations were formed to bring them to what passed for justice, by raising funds to pay for their trials. This was a common thing throughout the land. So here as elsewhere the landowners and the business community formed in 1813 the Ambleside Association for the Prosecution of Felons.

Gradually as police forces were formed, other communities allowed their redundant Associations to lapse. But in Ambleside the strong sense of history and tradition was not about to let that happen.

To this day, on a Wednesday in January, the town's business and tradesmen gather for a Dinner, followed by speeches, usually very humorous in the dry manner of the locality, followed by toasts to the monarch, the community and their Association. The proceedings are accompanied by a traditional menu, which hasn't changed since 1929, and much alcohol. Old friends who haven't met since last year's event converse together with much enthusiasm, bonds are renewed, friendships revived and a merry night is had by all. No one is recommended for arrest and prosecution. There are just fines for those members who fail to attend.

It has been suggested that with the decimation of the Police Force by State austerity programmes, the time may be approaching when the original functions of the Association will need to be revived.

# Ambleside Rushbearing

Usually taking place on the first Saturday in July, this is a festival celebration associated with the ancient custom of annually replacing the rushes on the earth floors of churches, rushes being a general term for rushes, reeds and sweet smelling grasses. Once widespread, very few places now continue this tradition.

AMBLESIDE RUSHBEARING

Although the church plays a leading role, today Rushbearing is also a community event. The bearings vary from large ornate devices such as hoops, staves and crosses to simple sheaves carried by children. Composed mainly of rushes cut from nearby lake shores, they are highly decorated with mosses, flowers and greenery. Large Church bearings, small church bearings, nursery and primary school children and clergy from all denominations set off from the primary school, accompanied currently by Burneside Brass Band. The procession continues up Compston Road and turns left at the top of the road, past the Bridge House and turns right up Smithy Brow – past the Golden Rule. Turning right into North Road the procession stops for a few minutes while the police allow the traffic which has been held up to go through the village. Setting off again the Procession continues through the streets to the Market Place. At this point everyone stops and raises their bearings – a great photo opportunity for the many onlookers. The traditional Ambleside Rushbearing Hymn is then sung and the Procession continues down Church Street to St. Mary's Church, arriving at about 3.15pm.

On arrival at St. Mary's the bearings are displayed around the church, where they remain throughout the services the following day. A short service of worship is held, then young participants are given a piece of delicious gingerbread on the way out of Church and then they collect a bag of food for their tea. Energy levels suitably topped up, families then make their way down to the School Playing field for the Rushbearing Sports – a traditional children's event organised by Ambleside's wonderful Fire Fighters and their families. All the usual races are held – flat and novelty – for each age group. This is followed by the Fell Race – the highlight of the Sports. This is Ambleside's prime Junior Fell Race now and the youngsters as young as seven or eight are justifiably proud of their times, racing up to Todd Crag and back.

It is advisable for visitors trying to travel through Ambleside on that day to avoid the village between 2.30pm. and 3.30pm. Why not come earlier and stay and watch?

From Ambleside Oral Archive, interviewee Joan Newby - born 1922, interviewed 2001:

Rushbearing was a huge thing for us because we didn't have many things really.

Was the Procession quite different to the procession that we are used to today or was it quite similar?

Well it - yes, it was the same, but much bigger and much - everybody had a new dress, everybody had new shoes, everybody dressed up which they don't now. We used to go and pick our flowers and grasses and make our own Rushbearings and they were all wooden crosses. Well - small ones, you had a basket with flowers in. But as you progressed, as you got bigger, it was a big thing you then had a cross. It was a wooden cross but on a base and we all made our own at home, covered in moss, rushes, grasses and flowers. There was a section for prize-giving for children who had made their own out of wild flowers. They all got books and they were judged by visitors who came. But it was all - it wasn't all on one day as it is today. Saturday was the Rushbearing Procession, took them to Church, had a Gingerbread, stayed in Church then. You collected your Rushbearings when you came out of school on Monday. And then after school was tea-party and sports. So it now it's all crowded onto one day and I'm not so sure that the children look forward to it like they did. But then you went into the Rushbearing until you were teenagers.

# Sports

Ambleside people have always been enthusiastic about sports. Traditionally, this sometimes involved the death of animals, especially in harder times when deer, foxes, moles, rabbits and badgers could severely damage vital crops and livestock, or were hunted for the pot. Other nowadays less excusable pastimes included dog fighting and cock fighting. Lakeland also has two sports you don't find elsewhere; hound trailing and wrestling (Cumberland & Westmorland style)

## Cockfighting

Cockfighting was made illegal in 1849. There is no hard evidence that it still takes place in central Lakeland, but highly secretive rural networks undoubtedly exist, mainly among travelling communities. A pair of metal cock spurs was made in Ambleside in the 1980s but that was for "display purposes".

## From Ambleside Oral Archive, interviewee George Braithwaite, born 1910, interviewed 1991

Now do you remember you once told me that you'd actually seen a cock fight?

I did yes.

Tell me about it.

Well I have quite a memory of it because I went with my father who was one of the game cock fighting fraternity as well as his father. And it was one Saturday morning I'd been with my father cutting some wood - coppice wood. I was only 9 years of age, and when we set off to work my father had two game cockerels in a sack, and I didn't ask questions because I wouldn't have got an answer. And we proceeded down to where my grandfather lived... Were there any bookies there, or was it all - there weren't any bookmakers?

No no no! It was a very very secret society was cock fighting: very secret, and you would never get anyone into conversation about cockfighting unless you knew them very well and they knew you. There was an old chap at Ambleside who was a Masterman Joiner, and he used to keep game birds, and they called him Flooty Mackereth. And I got to know that he was one of the game cock fighting fraternity, and it was months and months before he would talk to me although I made meself known to him that my father and grandfather were in the know of everything, but it was months before he would talk to me about cockfighting, and that was how secret the job was.

Now we're talking in 1993. Do you think there's any going on at all now?

Oh yes, there's quite a bit going on I think, one place an' another.

Up here in Cumbria?

I wouldn't like to say: but I understand there's quite a bit goes on at these big racing establishments: and in Ireland. So whether it's true or false now I wouldn't like to say for sure...

From the Ambleside Oral Archive, interviewee Laura Richardson, born 1907, interviewed 1985:

> You mention sport, one sport here was... Cockfighting, oh yes and hunting, fell-racing, wrestling.
> Do you remember all these things?
> Cockfighting I've never seen but I know there are places even now where it goes on, up Patterdale way, very secret.

## Fox hunting

The problem with fox hunting in Lakeland is whether it is a sport or a necessary means of protecting farm livestock, or both. It depends which side you are on, if any. The hunting of foxes with dogs was banned in 2005. While strongly held views for and against this ban occasionally surface locally, our resident pack of hounds is carefully maintained and exercised using dragged trails, to preserve the breed and in the hope that the ban may one day be repealed. Not many people appreciate the centuries of tradition and careful breeding that has gone into a pack of hounds, with meticulous records kept over many years. Prodigious feats of endurance are recalled about epic hunts in past years, many miles and feet of ascent often involved in a day's work by men and dogs. Hunting here was not a pastime for the mounted gentry, the chase taking place on the fells by working men on foot over miles of rough terrain.

## From the Ambleside Oral Archive, interviewee Cora Dixon, born 1893, interview 1983

No, the hunting dogs, they were up in the kennels here up in Greenbank. No, they were for the foxes. I remember – where was I, up Scandale, and Oh, a lovely fox just passed us like that. I never said a word. I was with him. Oh, they set up such a hullabaloo, these hounds. He said, "Did you see a fox?" "No". "Well, you must have, you were looking that way." "Well, I didn't see anything." I did. I saw a little fox looking out like that and they never got on the scent of it. Oh, I was so pleased! And another time I was out with them Under Loughrigg, before you come to those two houses. I was so intrigued because there was a man with a wooden leg and he was getting over the wall and I said,

"Can I help you?" And he said, "No, I can manage," and I said, "What's going on up in the wood?" And he said, "I think they've holed." "Oh," I said, "I'll get over myself." And I was so delighted, they were digging there and the fox had another run there. It got away! I was always so pleased when they got away. Oh, they're such pretty things, you know.

From the Ambleside Oral Archive, interviewee Bruce Logan, Master of Fox Hounds, born 1928, interviewed 2002:

How has the fox scene changed over the years?
Very little I would think. Rather more than there was if you went back to the '20s. If you went back to the '20s in the early part of the century, there were a lot of – three or four small estates where they employed a gamekeeper. Well after they ceased, the fox population began to grow.
What happened? The game-keeper was preserving his master's game birds? And so he would shoot and trap them?
Yes. Gamekeepers were very able at getting foxes. Very able really if they were a good keeper.

Once they'd gone have you then depended on the Lakeland packs to keep the foxes reasonably under control?

They've kept the foxes under control until the last 5 or 10 years. 5 years should I say: and then there's this other way of controlling foxes coming to be – that is using a gun and a lamp at night. Somebody discovered that _ though I don't know whether there's much of that used now– but somebody discovered a way of using a bit of polystyrene, and another bit of polystyrene that made a noise that there was a mating call of the dog and the vixen.

You mean rubbing them together?

Yes. Or you could do it by whistling I think somehow. I've never seen it done. And this resulted in them going at night and using that and a lamp. Shining a lamp about and if there were any foxes about it was attracted to this noise, and then they would shoot them. I don't know whether there's as much of that part going on, but there's an awful lot of shooting of foxes at night. This has really come partly by the manufacture of the very powerful lamps.

# Hound trailing

A trail hound is a lightweight foxhound, bred for speed rather than stamina, though not short of that either. Beginnings go back to the mid nineteenth century but the sport was not properly organised until the Hound Trail Association was formed in 1906. Prior to this all kinds of skulduggery went on to try and get a winner, laying false shortcuts or kidnapping rival hounds for instance or swapping dogs mid trail. The trails take place all summer all round the area. A trail is laid by men dragging a sack containing a solution of paraffin and liquid aniseed across the fells, over walls, crags, fences and other obstacles. The hounds are then released, running for 25 or 45 minutes depending on their age and experience, at up to average speeds of 20mph. They are kept lean and fit and trained to race back to their owners to receive a specially tasty feed, the recipes for which are kept secret. Pitfalls are several – the hounds need to be trained not to bunk off after a rabbit or a fox instead of sticking to the trail, nor to stop for a drink by a tempting little beck. As they come into view from the finishing line the excitement mounts to a crescendo of cries and whistles and bells as the owners yell encouragement to their hounds to make a final effort to win. Bookies are on hand to add to the drama of the event.

These events can be witnessed at Ambleside Sports each July and Rydal Hound Show in August, also at many other more remote venues throughout the Lake District.

## Fell Running

From its beginnings as a friendly competition between local mountain guides, this sport, which involves gruelling runs up steep fellsides and hair raising steep descents, has become a major Lakeland activity involving hundreds of entrants. More on this will be found later under the chapter on The New Sports. Meanwhile a watchful eye is kept on events involving masses of runners with their impact on footpath erosion and local communities.

# Cumberland & Westmorland Wrestling

## From Ambleside Oral Archive, interviewee Thomas (Tucker) Mason born 1931, interviewed 2002:

But the actual technique of the wrestling, is it different from any other?

Oh yes.

In what way?

Your back-holds, you see, one arm under and one arm over and you take a back hold and then you've different chips, which you apply with the rest of your body, your feet, your legs or whatever, which we call "chips", you see. You go various – you get your outside arms, your inside arms, your leg up buttocks, your full buttocks, your cross buttocks and then you've got your defences you see. A good wrestler is a good defensive wrestler with the move that he can – he knows his move, he knows his man's coming and you go against that, you see. He knows what's coming and...

That's right and he counteracts it, you see. Sometimes you can throw your opponent off the chip that he's coming with, you see. It's all what we call "in the knack".

What constitutes a win?

Oh, the first man that hits the ground with any part of his body above the knee. You can get a winning fall if you wrestle your opponent and you can pull him onto one knee if he's standing in that position, you can just pull him onto... he'll lose the fall with that but other than that, you know, it's any part of his body that hits the ground first above his knees.

Is that clear? Good! So you can put your new understanding of the complexities of this unique sport into practice at Ambleside Sports which is always held in Rydal Park on the last Thursday in July.

There you can also admire the traditional wrestlers' costume – a sleeveless vest, white long johns tucked into stockings and velvet trunks, often black, the backs of which are embroidered, traditionally by the wrestlers' wives or mothers, with floral designs in bright colours. There is a competition for the best designs and it is amusing to wonder what is going through the minds of the worthy lady judges as they slowly contemplate the rear end of these strapping young men.

CUMBERLAND AND WESTMORLAND WRESTLING

Similar back-hold style wrestling also takes place in Iceland and there have been contests between Lakeland men and Icelanders. This goes some way towards confirming the theory that the sport was introduced here by Norsemen in the 10th century.

Moving with the times, the sport's governing body has now introduced ladies' and girls' wrestling which may well mean more young lads will be tempted to train at the newly formed local wrestling academies.

## Sports and Social Clubs

Ambleside has men's and women's football teams and several youth teams. It has a thriving rugby union club, cricket club, also badminton, bowling, basketball and hockey clubs, as well as an athletics club.

In addition, at the last count there were also seventeen social and special interest organisations, including two Rotary clubs, choral, art, history, horticultural and charitable societies. It is a wonder anyone has time to go to work!

## The New Extreme Sports
- contributed by Dr Paul Davies, a keen participant and TriathlonX competitor.

In addition to our traditional sports and pastimes, in recent years Ambleside has become something of a centre for more extreme sporting events. The national trend towards endurance sport chimes well with efforts by the National Park Authority in seeking to promote the Lake District as an adventure venue. As this usually involves events drawing large numbers of participants and spectators, it has not gone down too well with those holding the more traditional view of the Lakes as a place for quiet enjoyment of peaceful landscape. Taking a more robust pragmatic view, Ambleside tends to support these crowd drawing events, which provide new commercial opportunities. Ambleside has the unique combination of lake proximity and extreme hill cycling and running right on its doorstep enabling such events to be planned in our beautiful surroundings.

## Outdoor swimming/wild swimming

Ambleside could justifiably claim to be the centre of outdoor swimming in the UK with a strong local scene and so far, the UK's only dedicated shop and training hub for open water swimming ("Swim the Lakes")

Opinions vary as to what is wild swimming as opposed to open water swimming, but "wild" fits the Ambleside scene with a few exceptions. It encompasses swimming in natural settings such as Rydal Water, Loughrigg Tarn, Grasmere or Windermere (tarns or lakes) or in becks or rivers such as Rydal Beck, Rothay or Brathay rivers. Favourite beaches and entry points abound for each, and variable esoteric terminology can be used to describe these – e.g. Buckstones Jum up in the Rydal Beck which is a nationally popular spot (a "jum" is technically a stretch of stream or beck that never freezes over).

Another colourful local name is "Dead Man's Dub", which is a deep pool in Easedale Beck in Grasmere. Why it is so named is currently unknown. It is now a favourite haunt for local swimmers and we hope for their sake that nowadays it will not live up to its name.

Locals and tourists alike wax lyrical about the joys of wild swimming, and the invigorating effects of swimming or floating in fresh water of varying temperatures – they swim all year round, in storms and breakers/white horses, as well as in the small section of Rydal Water that was unfrozen one New Year's Day. They say there is something special about being free from gravity and very much feeling in the moment when you are out there.

People swim in the early morning, with herons, ducks and otters, and throughout the day: others favour night swimming, often on a full moon evening, with barbeques and fires, with hot chocolate and whisky to follow. The word is spread quickly via social media.

Dress code varies from the staunchest skinny dippers (names and addresses available) to swimsuits and speedos, and finally wet suits (shorties and full suits). Respect is earned by the winter hardies who swim sans wetsuit – though a swim cap is considered *de rigeur* as well as goggles. Experiments in measuring body temperatures in swimmers variously clad have unsurprisingly shown the less you wear the colder your body will be, unless you're one of the zen masters who are able to generate a rise in their own body temperature to compensate for the water being bloody freezing....!!

Clearly there are risks of hypothermia although the options of wetsuit technology are now myriad to combat this; you can cheerfully spend a few hundred quid now on a swimming wetsuit with special panels to catch the water better and aid body rotation, as well as keeping you warm and make you look and feel slimmer! They are a battle to put on and removal is often facilitated by the prior application of body butter or products with names like "Body Glide" which are now available readily in Ambleside.

Chafing risks are ever present for the wetsuit wearer, but swimming naked can be hazardous too apparently, from legendary pike attacks, to having your clothing stolen from the shore or bank, or having the Bolton Rambling Club decide to eat their mid-morning snack at the point where you left your clothing.

BLOODY GREAT!

Naturally the purists shun wetsuits and the Long Distance Swimming Association ban them from most 'length of Lake Windermere' swims, although Vaseline is allowed...

The health benefits of outdoor swimming are those of lowering blood pressure and heart rates over time, as well as building muscles, and boosting metabolic rate – many people say they feel calmer and psychologically healthier with regular wild swimming and apparently it can boost libido also.

Wild swimming in the Ambleside area is internationally renowned, with several guidebooks featuring our local swim venues, and television programmes have featured these also.

Historically there is a long tradition of local wild swimming – with their love of bathing presumably the Romans at the Galava Fort swam at Waterhead. Older local Ambleside residents can recall the bathing hut which was there until the 1940s, with his and hers sections. The ruins can still just be seen.

The 'bibles' for local wild swimmers are William Heaton Cooper's *The Tarns of Lakeland* (1960), and John and Anne Nuttall's 1995 book of the same name. Latterly Kate Rew has written *Wild Swim*, and Daniel Start has written *Wild Swimming* – a guide to all the local venues (including some he was asked to leave out to avoid over-popularising them). Local swimmers also use the rivers, including the Rothay from White Moss then Rydal Water southwards to Lake Windermere.

## Swim-Hiking/Running

This has also begun locally, where you swim with a specially designed waterproof inflatable bag attached around your waist, with clothes kept dry within it. You can then swim across Lake Windermere, or the length of Rydal Water, and change back into dry clothes and continue your walk or run or dinner date. The competitive concept of the SwimRun has reached the area, where you swim in a short wetsuit and running shoes, then emerge and commence running immediately, without changing clothing at all.

The concept of swimming with an orange inflatable tow float, fixed around your waist, has really developed in latter years as a safety aid and was designed locally by Colin Hill of ChillSwim fame. It enables you to have a "rest" by holding on to the float if you wish to and also reduces your chance of being mown down by a lake cruise boat. Local junior schools have started open water swimming within the curriculum using these floats as part of the safety precautions. The more cynical observer has commented that these brightly coloured floats speed up the process of finding the deceased...

## The Great North Swim

2008 brought the Great North Swim to Ambleside, based at the Low Wood Hotel, and the concept has now spread to other UK venues. Now run over 3 days, thousands of swimmers from 12 years old upwards, can choose to swim half a mile up to 10km distance. Wetsuits are compulsory and swimmers wear a timing chip around their ankle, and swim between buoys. The event has continued annually, apart from when blue green algae stopped play one year, and wild weather another year.

Large amounts of money are raised for charity through the event, and many people begin their outdoor swimming journey here. And Ambleside is block booked for the weekend!! Last, but not least, is the annual ChillSwim, normally held in February, where wetsuits are not allowed and water temperatures are usually between 5-10 degrees c. The distances are shorter, within the Low Wood Marina and the participants are from all over the world.

It's all a far cry from the Romans dipping at Waterhead, but wild swimming is growing in popularity each year and Ambleside is at the hub of it all.

## Long Distance Running Events

## Brathay Marathon

Originally run in the 1980's, the Windermere Marathon was resurrected in 2006 as the Brathay Marathon, commencing at Brathay Hall, Ambleside. It is a full marathon, on roads and running all around Lake Windermere. It's a very hilly course and could easily be the most scenic course in the UK.

## Brathay 10 in 10

Each year a small group of runners attempt to run 10 marathons in 10 days, following the same course daily, and earning maximum respect and incredulity from all of Ambleside, as well as the horns of cars driving around the route! It really is a superhuman effort......with ice baths and massages at the end of each day as an option.

## Lakes 50 and 100

These 2 events usually start or pass through Ambleside, and cover either 50 or 100 miles of running/walking/limping on roads and trails through the Lake District... Ever more popular they sell out within hours and will always involve running through the night.

## Triathlon X

2016 brought a unique event to Ambleside for the first time, the brain-child of local lad Mark Blackburn. The world's toughest extreme triathlon, as analysed by triathlon magazines and forums alike, this IronMan distance triathlon involved swimming 2.4 miles at the head of Lake Windermere, then biking the famous Fred

Whitton Cycle Route which entails cycling 112 miles, with 12000 feet of ascent, and taking in the whole of the Lake District by cycling over all the passes, several with gradients of 25 per cent. The final part of the route was a 26 mile run along the Langdale Valley, then up to Esk Hause and Scafell Pike, the highest point in England (an overall climb of over 5000feet). Statistically it is the toughest course, in terms of the height gain on the bike route.

## Skyrunning 2016

This ultra running event started from Ambleside and the route ran all round the ridges of local mountains, hence running as near to the sky as possible.

## Long Distance Cycling Events

Various long distance cycling events (known as Sportives) commence in or pass through Ambleside, such as the Fred Whitton Cycle Ride, amongst the finest and toughest routes in the world as it climbs Kirkstone, Honister, Newlands, Whinlatter, Hard Knott and Wrynose passes along the 112 mile route. Over 2000 cyclists participate in this ride. Other rides all have enticing names such as the Christmas Cracker or Brathay Belter to encourage the middle aged men in lycra (MAMILS) to sign up. In 2017 the Brathay 262 was devised and entails cycling 10 laps of the Windermere Marathon course – 262 miles – to be completed within 24 hours (or not!).

## Kirkstone Car Pull

Usually in September, ladies' and men's teams pull a car 3 miles uphill from Ambleside, to the top of Kirkstone Pass, for local charities. It is of course pure coincidence that there is a pub at the finish. Incidentally, locally born people insist that it is only the last steep 300 yards of road before the pub that should be called 'The Struggle', not the entire road from Ambleside. So get that right, you latter day journos!

## No Wood Low Wood Cardboard Boat Race

This quirky boating event requires teams to build a boat from cardboard and paper alone then sail/row it from the Low Wood Hotel, for as long as possible before it inevitably sinks....and the crew must wear fancy dress.

# CHAPTER 10

# Wildlife – Flora and Fauna

It has to be said that Ambleside is not Cumbria's most exciting nature reserve. It is far too busy these days and much of the wildlife of even 50 years ago has disappeared. Factors other than tourism have also had their effect. Hen and stag parties plus student revels may be the only signs of 'wildlife' obvious to the casual observer. However, if you know how and when to watch wildlife you can be rewarded with local sightings of some less common animals and birds. You don't see these if you talk or move about a lot. You need to find likely places and sit quietly at the right times, letting the fauna come to you. Early mornings bring the best chances.

## Birds

Some species of waterfowl have been bullied out of the area by excessive numbers of Canada geese, others by predation by mink. We rarely if ever see coots, pochard, grebe or goldeneye on local waters. These were fairly common until recently. The population of small birds has fluctuated. More sparrows, less chaffinches, more nuthatches, less swifts – theories abound on the causes – there are more nest raiding pirates such as jays and magpies and some blame badgers for the decline of ground nesting species.

But along the Rivers Brathay and Rothay, there are still dippers, a kingfisher or two, grey wagtails, herons. In the woods, pied and spotted flycatchers can still be seen in late spring and summer. Green and greater spotted woodpeckers are common, while the lesser spotted has disappeared. Among rarer species, whooper swans, woodcock, snipe and water rail are seen occasionally at the right time of year. On Loughrigg, the skylark and curlew have gone but the cuckoo abounds, plonking its eggs in the nests of meadow pipits and dunnocks who are too daft to kick its unruly offspring out. In the town, pigeons and jackdaws are too numerous to be welcome.

Of raptors, gardens are visited by sparrowhawks. Buzzards, often mobbed by crows, are common overhead, as are kestrels and peregrine falcons. Very rarely a golden eagle or a goshawk is seen and occasionally one of the re-introduced red kites.

In spring and autumn oystercatchers pass overhead at night, on their way to or from their moorland breeding grounds. You hear them, twittering away in the darkness to keep in touch. On spring mornings, skeins of geese pass over the Rothay valley, honking mournfully, moving between the local lakes.

## Mammals

We have the secretive and elusive stoats and weasels, plenty of mice, voles, moles and rats. Otters have made comeback in some local rivers and lakes. You are very likely to see badgers - they regularly raid the litter bins at night in Rothay Park. Someone needs to teach them a bit of road sense, along with the hedgehogs. In the woods at dusk and early dawn you will see roe deer and the occasional red. The numbers of roe are 'getting out of hand' according to some, likewise badgers. Rabbit numbers fluctuate as ever with bouts of myxomatosis. The red squirrel is staging a bit of a comeback, assisted by enthusiastic culling of the greys, who have only reached the Lakes over the past twenty years. The reds are shy. You may find them in the woodland between Rydal and Grasmere if you're very patient and still. They regularly visit local gardens where food is offered.

## Fish

The best way to find out about fish in local waters is to be an angler and buy a guest permit from the Windermere, Ambleside and District Angling Association. Trout, pike, perch, roach and eel are popular prey, though the trout population is in decline.

The population of rare arctic char in Windermere, a local delicacy once plentiful, has declined in recent decades along with the number of char fishermen, with their unique char boats and trolling technique. Several reasons are suggested for its demise, including loss of breeding grounds and poor water quality. Schemes are proposed now to improve the treatment of waste water from the locality and reduce the amount of phosphates entering the lake by encouraging more responsible use of household products and agricultural fertilisers. Too many dishwashers in holiday homes are apparently just part of the problem – use eco-friendly detergents!

## Trees

If you look at old landscape paintings and photographs, you will realise how many once open views are now completely obscured by unmanaged woodland. Landowners' inaction has allowed tree growth, which used to be valued for coppicing, fuel and charcoal, to burgeon uncontrolled. Many lovely views which used to be available from the valleys can now only be seen from high on the fells. Perhaps 'National Park' is becoming a misnomer – National Forest will be more appropriate before too long.

Nearby there are some spectacular examples of fine trees. A walk through Rydal Park will show you some fine old native specimens. And just south of Waterhead you will find a magnificent wood containing even larger trees, including the tallest tree in Cumbria. It is a Grand Fir which at the time of writing stands 58m high (190ft). It is on National Trust land in a Victorian arboretum called Skelghyll Woods. Take the drive off the A591 signposted to Stagshaw Garden. It's not far, just a short walk from Waterhead. Visit Stagshaw too, especially in spring for its spectacular collection of rhododendrons and azaleas.

## Flowers

Wildflowers abound, on the fells, in the woods – primroses, violets, wood anemones, wood sorrel, celandines, birdsfoot trefoil, harebells, common orchid, bistort, burnet, clover, foxgloves, buttercups and daisies... all sorts flower throughout the seasons. In spring there are some superb carpets of bluebells, such as in the woods near Grasmere and at Jiffy Knots at Brathay. The late flowering and invasive Himalayan balsam continues to appear despite eradication attempts. Wild fruits such as bilberries, sloes, blackberries and raspberries are common.

In boggy and in damper areas you will find bog asphodel, bog orchid, and the insectivorous sundew. Fungi thrive in sparse fellside woodland, boletus being common. The red toadstool fly agaric can be found and in secret locations such as in woodland on the lower slopes there are sought after fungi such as chanterelles.

# CHAPTER 11
# Tales of old Ambleside

## The old roads

Before the mid eighteenth century, not many people bothered to come to Ambleside. (Some local residents who don't need to make a living here would be quite happy if that were still the case.) Not many local folk at that time would have much reason to travel anyway. The community was virtually self-sufficient and what essentials couldn't be got here would be brought in by travelling pedlars. Mostly, if it wasn't grown, bred, caught or made here people did without it. Perhaps there's a lesson there concerning our excessive consumption today.

Anyway, pedlars, officials and other travellers would arrive in the village from the south via Waterhead using an old Roman causeway which was raised above what was then marshland. Mary Armitt in her article 'Ambleside Town & Chapel' of 1905 suggests that the main route to the Market Square from the causeway followed present day Compston Street and The Slack.

Rudimentary accommodation was available at several inns, including the Black Cock (then the Commercial, now the Queens), Salutation, the Royal Oak and White Lion. The only road north was somewhat unoriginally named North Road, probably wider than it is now. You then turned left at the crossroads after passing present day Garside's Butcher, down Smithy Brow, turning right into Nook Lane. From here the traveller reached what is now Nook End, until recently a farm, whence a track now lost went left along the fell, above Rydal Hall, to join what is now known, and probably was then, as the coffin road. This approached Grasmere by way of Dove Cottage.

The route west from Ambleside went via Clappersgate and Little Langdale, following the old Roman route over Wrynose and Hardknott passes.

The coffin, or corpse, road was so called because it was used to carry the dead to Grasmere for burial. Interment in sacred ground was thought essential and Ambleside had only a chapel of ease. Along the route there were several resting places, large platform slabs where the weary bearers could lay the coffin and rest a while. One still remains in place. It is said, and there is no reason to disbelieve it, that after having rested first at the Golden Rule and/or the Fox and Goose before even setting off, such long rests were necessary as resulted in coffins often arriving in Grasmere very late for the burial ceremony.

ON THE COFFIN TRAIL

As previously mentioned, after much agitation, a chapel, St Anne's, was built at How Head in Ambleside, which no doubt made funerals less onerous but also less of a good day out.

## The circus comes to town

From Ambleside Oral Archive – interviewee Percy Middleton, born 1904, interviewed 1981:

Oh yes we played circuses because in those days each summer all the circuses used to come touring round and come to Ambleside. They were in Rothay Park there: and there was one of the circuses called Sanders, there was this big menagerie ~ which was entirely like a big zoo on wheels, as you might say, because they came in the park and they set them out in a big square and of course you had to pay an entrance to go in and see all these animals and watch when they put all the lions into one big cage where the lion tamer went in with them: and then there was another called Bill's Wild West Circus also used to come and there we used to see "the attack on the Deadwood Mail": with the coach galloping round and the Indians chasing after it on their horses and there were sort of imitation fire

going inside and the cowboys firing blank cartridges
you know and of course we lapped that up."

## School days

From Ambleside Oral Archive - Percy Middleton,
born 1904, interviewed 1981:

> What happened if you weren't there at nine o'clock in
> the morning? Well you got the cane: one stroke across
> each hand you know. It depends how late you were,
> and how often you were late: if you were very late or
> often late well then you got two. Or perhaps you were
> kept in: you know at midday he'd say oh you stop here
> a while. At night time you were kept in at school.

From Ambleside Oral Archive - interviewee Dorothy
Barrow, born 1906, interviewed 1996:

> One of the girls told my father that some of the boys
> were going into the Co-operative Stores at lunch
> time and filling their pockets with toffees whilst
> the assistant went to get their order. My father was
> very indignant but when the boys were accused, they
> said - shall we say - "Smith and Jones started it
> all and of course, they're up at the Quarry working,

now". My father sent up to the Quarry Master and said could he see Smith and Jones. Smith and Jones came down – my father put all the culprits in a row and caned the whole lot of them and no objection was made by the Quarry Master or the parents – it was accepted as the right thing to do. I don't think education would stand for that today.
So he caned even the boys who had left the school?
Yes.

## The Fire Brigade

From Ambleside Oral Archive – interviewee William Nicholson, born 1898, interviewed 1978:

Tell me about the fire service then, when did all that start?
Since I was a young fellow I was in the fire service.
It was called Windermere Fire Service?
No it was Ambleside Fire Service. We were the best in the district. I'll show you a picture of it.
What year would it have been that you joined?
Well I was married in 1928...
What sort of machine did you have then?

Well we had the old... well we had a steamer, it went by steam, it was a motor car but the pump was worked by steam... and we used to do our competition drill on an old manual, we used to pump it, it was only used for competition work. We were very efficient – we used to get there before the fire had started nearly! The pride of Westmorland.

How did you take part in competitions? Oh yes, we went up to Cumberland and all round Westmorland, we used to get all the prizes.

How did you call people to the fire station?

There's a bell where the Mechanics is, there used to be a bell on top of that, the firebell. Anyone, first to the fire bell got five shillings.

Five shillings for ringing the fire bell?

Yes, that used to rouse us you see until the war came and then we all had bells fixed in our houses.

How many were in the brigade?

Twelve.

How were you paid?

Two pounds a year, retaining fee. And now they get – I don't know what they get.

Did you get more for each fire?

*It depends, the bigger the fire the better the money.*

*How could you tell how big the fire was, how did they judge it?*

*Well you got the signal to the fire and as you went there, it just depends how it burnt you see, if it's just a small fire well you were only there so long and you were paid by the hour, well if it was a big fire you were alright.*

*So it meant if you were longer...*

*...You see the majority of the firemen were tradesmen and if they left their work you see they got their money stopped then so they had to get it out of the fire service.*

## Stock Beck and Stock Ghyll

For the purpose of this book, Stock Ghyll starts at the waterfalls in Stock Ghyll Park and Stock Beck ends at Miller Bridge by Rothay Park where it joins the River Rothay. Where the Ghyll becomes the Beck is not clear and the use of the term River Stock by some people doesn't help. Whatever, this waterway was once the lifeblood of the community, serving many purposes. Obviously a fresh water source, it was also a sewer, a rubbish tip, a fishery and a power source for the many waterwheels which drove the mills of the town. The beck also marked the boundary between the ancient jurisdictions of Grasmere and Windermere. The original community north of the beck was 'Above Stock', south was 'Below Stock'. Obvious landmarks

on the beck are the Bridge House, already mentioned, and the reach of the beck between the upper bridge in North Road and the lower bridge on Rydal Road on which you can still see the old boundary stone on the parapet. This reach contains a replica of the old corn mill waterwheel, attached to what is now the 'Giggling Goose' café. This replica is the second one, the first having been made by Brian Jackson during the period when the property was home to the famous Old Mill Pottery which operated from 1948 to the 1980s. The mill race was once continued across a conduit above the beck to drive a bark mill on the opposite side of the beck, beautifully illustrated in a painting by J M W Turner. That wheel is long gone but the property remains as a sheepskin shop, entered from Bridge Street. The riverside garden, now somewhat neglected, was beautifully maintained until 2005 by Fred Vergauwen (1911–2007), old radical thinker, geologist, artist and gardener. There is a plaque in his memory on the wall just inside the gate from Rydal Road. There stands a rare dawn redwood tree, unusual in that they are conifers but deciduous. It was also the shady site of old Fred's beloved perennial giant hogweed, the presence of which he successfully concealed from the authorities who would undoubtedly have removed it on health and safety grounds. Fred tended the plant, carefully removing its seeds each autumn to prevent it spreading.

Amusement can be had in enquiring why Stock Beck and Stock Ghyll are so called. There are two offerings. The upper length of the beck, above the town towards the waterfalls, was home to a watermill which powered a bobbin factory. Lower down were fulling and bark mills. Fulling is the process by which woollen cloth is cleaned and thickened. This is done mechanically in a mill by hammering the wet cloth, the hammers being called stocks. So you might think the origin of the name is obvious.

However, it is said that in the grounds surrounding what is currently the Rock Shop in North Road (previously Palfreyman's plant shop), where the upper corner alongside the road meets the beck wall, stood the village stocks where naughty people were trapped and pelted with nasty things in punishment for their transgressions, of which there were many in bygone times. Hence the name, Stock Beck, into which would fly any badly aimed missiles. Probability would suggest prosaically which of these offerings is the more likely. But which is the more fun to believe?

Incidentally, before mills were used for fulling, it was done by the laborious tread of human feet, at which time it was also called 'walking' or 'tucking'. So if your name is Walker, Tucker or Fuller, you know what your great great granddad did for a living.

From Ambleside Oral Archive, interviewee Theo Stephenson, born 1917, interviewed 1991:

What else? We know the Market Cross has been moved, were there any stocks?

Yes, there were stocks. You can still see the stocks 'slab' where the stocks stood by Palfreymans shop there, just on Stock Bridge, hence the name. The stocks stood there and if you look over the wall just as you get past the entrance to – if you're walking up towards North Road, just past the entrance to Palfreymans Garden Centre, [now the Rock Shop] you'll see a big slab of stone there, where the stocks stood on.

Yance ower, (time was when) Stock Beck was dubbed Butcher Beck. This was because it was used as a way of fortuitously fattening the fish in Windermere. In those days, the local hotels kept stables and there were hundreds of horses in Ambleside. When these animals had reached the end of their useful life, through exhaustion, accidents, old age etc., they were slaughtered and the unwanted innards were dumped into the beck, probably joined by some butchers' waste. It is to be hoped they waited till the beck was in spate.

More recently, when the water was high the beck was used by Kirkstone Quarry to empty its holding tanks of slate slurry. This turned the water to a milky white, sometimes for days. Not many fish come up to the town nowadays, maybe their ancestors couldn't see where they were going and the route has been lost to fishy memory.

Years ago the bed of the beck under the Bridge House was regularly dredged by local builders to get the gravel and sand that accumulated there. That made the beck much deeper at that point and it was a haunt of large trout, sea trout and salmon. These fish could get upstream to spawn as far as the weir in Stock Ghyll park. Smaller fish can still be seen sometimes. But the days when it was worth fishing ended a few decades ago. In those days in the weeks before Christmas, a bit of naughty nighttime fishing was done to provide a festive fat specimen. Beyond is the bridge into Rydal Road car park. This was in ancient times a ford known traditionally as Halicar, which presumably led to a track towards what is now Stony Lane and the river. The present car park bridge was scheduled to be widened in 2013 but after a lot of work was done, the unforeseen cost of reinforcing the opposite bank against flood waters led to the project being halted. So next time you're held up entering the car park, ask the district council what their next move is.

Beyond the car park the beck runs into a walled channel for the rest of its course into the river. Part of its natural course was previously across Rothay Park, then owned by Colonel Rhodes. He lived at Rothay Holme (now Ambleside Manor guest house) and was a bit of a philanthropist. He used to devise projects to employ local men during winters when they were often laid off their regular work. One of these projects was to divert the beck into this new walled channel. This helped to drain the previous course from the marshy land which became Rothay Park after it was presented by the colonel to the local authority. Good on him!

# The Market Cross

The upright stones of this cross, now outside the Post Office in Central Buildings are ancient and go back to the granting of Ambleside's Market Charter in 1650.

The cross has moved about a bit. It used to be roughly where Barclays Bank is. Or was. The bank closed in 2014, following HSBC's example the previous year. The stones disappeared for some years and were found half buried in the grounds of the house known as

MARKET CROSS

Stepping Stones, Underloughrigg. This was occupied at the time by the Wordsworth people. Maybe one of them took the stones home for safe keeping while a new site was found. Then died.

From Ambleside Oral Archive, interviewee William Thornborough, born 1919, interviewed 1991:

Tell me about the old mill and the market cross.

Well the market cross has been moved and it was supposed to have been erected by one of the Redmaynes in 1872 but, to me, it doesn't make sense, because it was elsewhere, it hasn't been always there. It's been there a long time I think but old prints show that it was farther down. Now I think the site would be about where Martin's Bank door would be originally, somewhere about there. Now the Mechanics Institute with the clock tower, that was given by one of the Harrisons of Green Bank, you see. He built that in 1863 and he built 'em a courtroom the year after and he gave it over to what is the Ambleside Charity Trustees to maintain but he built it out of his own money and there's all sorts of things like that. And that was built in 1863 — I used to think it might just have been about there – but if that was built in 1863 and the cross was put to its present position in 1872, it couldn't have been there, it would have been moved in 1863. So it must have been about where the Martin's Bank – or Barclays Bank I should say now – where their doorway is, somewhere there...

Are there any bits of Ambleside that have managed to really stay the way they were – bits of things that have really been there 3–400 years – what about the Market Cross for instance?

The Market Cross, well you know that's been moved 3 times that I know of.

Where was it originally?

Where did the Market Cross start?

It stood more or less in the middle of the road on the top of the hill there, you know looking into the Market Square without putting it onto a screen you can't very well visualise it because the buildings have been changed so much in that area.

Was that where the market was held?

Oh yes that was where the market was held.

Was it a Wednesday market?

It was a Wednesday market yes. The first market charter was in 16... now then: 1660 something, and then there was another charter came out in 1688. Certainly William Green's guide to the Lake District about 1800 describes it as a Wednesday market. Oh yes. And still is today, the market charter is still in existence and it should be, whether it is or not I don't know, it should be in the possession of Barclays Bank. They should have it somewhere. Whether they have or not is the question – but it was in Martins Bank previous to that.

It ought to be in the record office in Kendal now.

Not long ago a local benefactor kindly embellished the cross, placing a specially commissioned sundial on top of it, as there used to be in bygone days. It disappeared almost overnight.

The granting of a Market Charter distinguishes a settlement from a village or a town. Most Ambleside residents like to think they live in a village. They refer to it as the village, not the town. Others think it is a town because it has a Market Charter. But if the definition 'market town' means having rights concerning self-government, it ain't no town.

At the timing of writing, the Market, held on a Wednesday in the car park opposite the Library, is nothing to get excited about. In winter it's likely only two traders will turn up. But for their sake, the whole badly needed car park is closed to cars. So the Local Council, who rely on car park revenues to an excessive degree, would be wise to try move the Market somewhere else.

# CHAPTER 12

# Nearby places

## Clappersgate & Brathay

The visiting motorist heading off to Hawkshead, Coniston or Langdale will probably whizz through Clappersgate. It's where you can turn left for Hawkshead, over that awkward narrow bridge called Brathay Bridge at which you probably have to give way to approaching traffic.

WHICH WAY TO BRATHAY PLEASE?

But little do those hurrying through know! Firstly, few people know whether at this spot they are in Brathay or Clappersgate. Probably you are in Clappersgate unless you cross the river, in which case you may be in Brathay. So what is Clappersgate? And what is Brathay?

Clappersgate is the group of houses you pass through as you approach that left turn to Hawkshead but carry straight on. More a hamlet than a village, having no shop, no pub (although it once had three) it consists only of mostly rather large expensive houses strung out along the road and beyond the junction. The problem is that some of the houses on this road think they are in Brathay... At some point further along the road you leave Clappersgate and enter Skelwith but we don't know where.

The most prominent of these Clappersgate houses is the Croft. On an elevated site it is visible from the south for miles. Once a humble cottage, it was transformed into a palatial mansion, now apartments, by a sugar tycoon called James Branker in the early 19th century. The property has riverside gardens on the opposite side of the road, once connected by a footbridge.

The Croft

From Ambleside Oral Archive, interviewee Joan Dutton, born 1918, interviewed 1988:

There was a cousin of mine, Pippin and I. This cousin was the same age group, and we would have lovely games on our own, and then we would go across this bridge that led down to the lower garden having been told not to spit on the cars below – which we did of course, these lovely open cars which went past, and down below there was this gorgeous garden which led down to the river, and there were boats and although we were very little we were allowed out in these boats, and we'd go down on to Windermere and row up the river and just do what we wanted all day.

Those children on their way to the lake would have passed Mr Branker's other property, the Boathouse. Here, where the Brathay and the Rothay rivers meet, was once the Roman landing place for Galava Fort. A few years prior to its acquisition by Mr Branker it was painted and drawn by William Green and John Harden, showing it with a jetty, cargo, pleasure craft and a kiln. The jetty handled slate and charcoal for shipment down Lake Windermere and imported gunpowder for the local quarries.

From Ambleside Oral Archive, interviewee Mary Hallatsch, born 1912, interviewed 1983:

> Yes, and she tells me about the time that they had to make butter, and there was this great big sink they had to scrub clean before they made it. They did all that at The Croft, they had their own farm and all the butter was made. Then about the housekeeper – and they'd had a marvellous big party, and she sent in the trifle – no it was fruit and cream, she said, that was it, and it went in and it all came out, and they didn't know what was the matter. And she'd put salt in instead of sugar. And

she nearly got sacked for that. Mother hadn't but the housekeeper had.

# Brathay

Legally Brathay is an ecclesiastical parish. Or it was until 1967 when it was absorbed by Ambleside. Brathay is also a bridge. And a river. And a church. And a manorial hall. And a quarry. And it's got Jiffy Knots up Bog Lane. However, most visitors see none of these because apart from a gravelly layby on the right by the river, there is nowhere to park.

The River Brathay starts up in the fells at the Three Shires Stone. It flows through Little Langdale Tarn, Elterwater and Skelwith, thence via Brathay to Lake Windermere. Prior to the creation of the county of Cumbria in 1974 the river was the boundary between Westmorland and Lancashire. When you crossed Brathay Bridge you were in Lancashire, but you didn't feel any worse off, or better.

During World War 2, an enemy alien, a German, visited Ambleside. It was the nearest he could get to his girlfriend who lived in Hawkshead and worked at Wray Castle when it was used by the Freshwater Biological Association. He wasn't permitted to be in Lancashire.

From Ambleside Oral Archive, interviewee Vernon David, a German classified as enemy alien, born 1920, interviewed 2008:

Well, I had the first opportunity of coming up North, from London, in July 1942, hoping to visit Joan, but I was not allowed to visit Wray Castle at that time because, oddly enough, Wray Castle was part of Lancashire. The whole of the West side of Windermere was on – belonged to Lancashire, whereas Ambleside was in Westmorland and all of the Langdale valley was in Westmorland as well, so a boundary between Westmorland and Lancashire at that time was the bridge over the River Brathay, in Clappersgate. So the best I could do, and I was allowed to do – with some difficulty but I did have permission from the police – was visit Clappersgate where I stayed in a B and B. But I was not allowed to go beyond the bridge.

The reason why you couldn't go beyond the bridge was what?

Well because there was a German Prisoner-of-War Camp at Grisedale and it was territory that aliens – friendly or otherwise – were not allowed to visit.

Okay, so, in other words, Joan Storey had to come and visit you in Clappersgate?

Yes, she came, the only way we could meet was for her to cycle the 5 miles from Wray Castle to Clappersgate.

From Ambleside Oral Archive, interviewee Marjorie Acheson, born 1886, interviewed 1980:

I don't know if you know that hymn, "O Perfect Love?" Yes. Well when my Uncle Hugh was married at Brathay Church in 1882, his bride's sister Dorothy Plumfield wrote that hymn for their wedding. Really? Yes, and the second time it was sung was at Brathay Church when our parents were married. And some years after that it got into the hymn book.

# Brathay Hall

BRATHAY HALL

In the 18th century someone called George Law, whose family had an interest in Backbarrow ironworks, built Brathay Hall, a Georgian-style country mansion set on a 360 acre property overlooking Lake Windermere. The property was later rented to John Harden, an amateur artist who lived a life of leisure, entertaining the local intelligentsia, guests such as poets William Wordsworth and Samuel Taylor Coleridge. Romantic landscape painter John Constable also visited.

In 1833, the property was sold to Giles Redmayne, who made his money as a draper dealing in Indian silk. Five years later he built Brathay Church. His descendants lived at the estate for almost a century.

Redmayne's great grandson Martin Redmayne was a politician who was created a life peer, becoming the first of the Redmayne baronets. The Redmayne family owned the estate until Francis Scott, founder of the Provincial Insurance Company based in Kendal, purchased the property in 1939. In the late 1990s a descendant of the Redmaynes contributed to the restoration of Brathay Church bells.

Francis Scott was a philanthropist who had bought the estate to protect it from development. Looking for a useful purpose for it, he founded the Brathay Hall Trust, to offer holidays to young people with an emphasis on a range of activities, including boating, fell-walking, camping, art and drama. Later this developed into today's functions, which encompass management training and tourist accommodation which subsidise outdoor courses for disadvantaged city based young people, introducing them to the great outdoors.

# Rydal

The hamlet of Rydal has a rich history. It has changed little in the last 100 years, being largely a privately owned estate.

As you travel north along the A591 you will pass the entrance to Ambleside Cricket Club (incidentally regarded as one of England's most beautiful grounds). Immediately beyond this on the left is a rocky tree clad knoll, its extent invisible from the road. Here we may begin this brief but rich history.

This knoll, with an aspect nearly from Windermere Lake to beyond Rydal Water, formed a fine lookout point for the Roman armies as they fought to subdue the local tribes and establish a route northward. Prior to that, Celts and Britons dwelt hereabouts.

Centuries later the original Rydal Hall occupied this site, a humbler dwelling by far than its grandiose successor. Recorded history begins in 1295 but we won't go that far back. 'Modern' Rydal could be said to begin with the acquisition of the manor by the Le Flemings, whose ancestors were Normans and who still own much of the area. Daniel le Fleming came in 1575 to the original "Old Hall". The family then set about acquiring local land and properties and during the following centuries ended up with most or all of it, their crowning glory being the gradual development of the present Rydal Hall. Predatory and harsh treatment of the local tenant farmers by earlier generations of the Le Flemings was something later generations mitigated, building the church and a free school. Later still a hydro electric generator was installed and supplied the village. Still enjoyed today are the 150 year old trees the family planted along the drive through their park, now a public bridleway. Nevertheless, the estate until recently was somewhat feudal in its administration by the Le Flemings.

At one time the village had five small farms, several water powered mills, a smithy and three inns.

Prominent ancient buildings today are 16th century Rydal Lodge, previously the Hare and Hounds, Rydal Mount (Wordsworth's home, open to the public) and Undermount. There is speculation that the mound between these latter two houses may have been raised and used as an ancient tribal meeting place.

From Ambleside Oral Archive, interviewee Tom Gibson, born 1904, interviewed 1986:

> Things were very restricted, fields, rivers, the lake was looked upon as a God given right to the Le Flemings and we were ordered off his property if seen. The front drive in my young days was a private drive for the use of the Le Flemings only. The Le Flemings were never closely involved with the villagers, only to order any washing that was on the line to dry, had to be taken down if they were walking past the house. The young ones had to raise our hats...

From Ambleside Oral Archive, interviewee Margaret Fuller, born 1926, interviewed 2007:

> ...and then there was a story that Eddie told; the road up from the main road was not tarmacked until very late on and in bad weather, times of flooding, a lot of the sammell which was what they put on would run, would flow down the hill and have to be brought back up and re-sited in wheelbarrows.

And one day Tom had been doing this job and had come up to, up the back drive which was slightly higher than the way you came in to the front door at Rydal Hall, and he just put this barrow down to have a slight breather because it was hard work, and there were some steps up by the front door, when the old squire had come up these steps and said 'Er, Gibson, what are you doing?' and he said, 'I'm just having a rest', and he said 'Right, you can pick up your cards, you're fired'.

Rydal Hall is now a conference centre owned by the Diocese of Carlisle. The fine formal gardens and grounds, with tea room, are open to the public.

## Cote Howe

If you cross the little Pelter Bridge from the A591 and turn right there is a little car park (you pay). Don't be tempted to go straight ahead instead to park on the meadow either side of the road beyond the bridge. The farmer will definitely deal with you sternly if you do. Beyond the little car park the road continues to Rydal Lake and is one of the area's most popular walks.

COTE HOW

Almost immediately you reach a fine old residence called Cote Howe, now a venue for weddings and special events. The site was known to the Romans and may have formed part of their road towards Keswick. The house dates from the 16th century and has an original spinning gallery. It was once a farm. The artist Fred Yates stayed here and it was also here that he painted a portrait of Woodrow Wilson, later US President.

# Stock Ghyll Park and Waterfalls

In Victorian times these were a major attraction as there wasn't much else to do. The land was privately owned and maintained and a charge made to visit the falls, more if you rode there on a hired donkey. Now it is owned by the District Council and there is no charge and it is rather neglected. Nonetheless it is beautiful and peaceful and well worth a visit. Don't expect Niagara – our falls are on a scale more in keeping with the Lakeland environment. The best time to view them is after rain in winter or spring before the surrounding uncontrolled tree growth severely restricts the aspect from the obvious viewpoints. You could be forgiven for making a comparison with the Amazon rain forest at such times. Moves are currently in hand to try to remedy this situation. Even better is when the falls are frozen solid but this a rare event nowadays.

# CHAPTER 13

## A Historical Background

An early tourist

Ambleside's history goes back at least to the Romans, the Vikings (who gave us our local place names) and to Charles Dickens who had this to say in Household Words; "Round Ambleside you will indeed find hills and waterfalls – decked with greasy sandwich papers and porter bottles, and the hills echo with the whistles of the Windermere steamers... brass bands play under your hotel windows, char-a-bancs, wagonettes and brakes of all colours rattle about with cargoes of tourists who have been 'doing' some favourite round. Touts pester you in the streets and in the hotel coffee room you overhear a gentleman ask angrily "Why don't they build an 'ut on 'elvellyn – they've got one on Snowdon."

A popular misconception is that Ambleside has a solely rural past. It was in fact highly industrialised, involved heavily in the production of charcoal, used in smelting the iron ore of Furness and west Cumbria, then timber for the production of bobbins for the textile industry. It adopted water power at an early stage and later developed machine tool manufacture. Quarrying and mining were local industries, and quarrying continues to be, despite attempts by conservationists to stop it, an interesting case of blinkered thinking — we are forced to use local slate and stone for building.

The town thus played a full part in the industrial revolution. But to go even further back, to possibly just beyond the memory of our native elders:

## Romans

It was not until the first century AD that man left archaeological evidence of his presence in Ambleside. This is provided by the Roman remains of Galava, a fort and settlement in the meadows at the head of Lake Windermere which we now call Waterhead. Here there are extensive remains of the fort, its first version being built in about 90 AD, later to be extended by Hadrian. In various excavations many artefacts have been found in the surrounding fields. The Armitt Museum has much information on this Roman site.

Galava had road links to Hardknott fort in Eskdale and thence to the major Roman port at Ravenglass on the west coast. From Galava a road also ran northwards, via Troutbeck and over the fell known as High Street, towards Penrith and the farthest outpost of the Empire, Hadrian's Wall. In recent years much research has gone into the possibility that another Roman road existed to Keswick following roughly the line of the A591. It has been more or less established that this route did exist, leaving Ambleside Galava Fort by way of the Rothay valley.

## Middle Ages and Vikings

The Romans were here until the gradual decline of their Empire. Some time between 300 and 400 AD they left England, though by that time only high ranking military staff and administrators would have been native Romans. What was left behind and what ensued when the rule of Rome collapsed we can only imagine. The Dark and Middle Ages saw fragmentation of territories and the division of Britain into warring tribal kingdoms, with the Church remaining and developing as the one unifying element, the monasteries later to become centres of ecclesiastical and economic power.

# Ambleside Develops - 1000 to 1700 AD

Being part of Scotland, Cumbria was not included in the Doomsday book. It became part of England following invasion in 1092 by William II. During the next 900 years, Ambleside and its surroundings grew as an industrial centre, but remained distant and inaccessible to the rest of Britain. In relative isolation, it avoided much of the Scottish raiding during the border wars and there is no record of plagues. The 'old' town of Ambleside, on the hill surrounding St Anne's Chapel (now apartments) was built after the Romans left, using some stone taken from the Roman fort at Galava. Gradually the town extended during the 16th and 17th centuries into the area below Stock Beck which has become the centre today. Mining activity expanded. Expert miners came from Germany and Wales in Elizabethan times to help exploit the rich copper veins at Coniston, thus the local people learned new skills. Copper was found in large amounts, also lead, though the larger deposits were not in the immediate area of Ambleside. Slate quarrying, which had always supplied local building needs, became a major export industry, while farming sustained a population almost self-sufficient in food production, though diet was not very diverse. In addition to sheep, cattle and pigs, oats and barley were grown and a variety of wild plants eaten. Other cereals and vegetables did not grow well in the poor soil of the wet and stony valleys, aggravated by long winters and short summers.

The dissolution of the monasteries by Henry VIII led to major changes in local land ownership and tenure, with most of it divided into small farms by 1550, owned or rented by local people. A market charter was granted in 1650, adding to the town's modest prosperity, and a successful trade developed in cloth, bark, corn and paper. In 1723 an educational trust was set up in the will of John Kelsick to start a school for boys.

## Industrial Revolution

As the industrial revolution gathered pace across England, the canal system reached Kendal, linking it to Preston in Lancashire. The Napoleonic wars with their adverse effect on imports, had a major impact on wool production, with every inch of grazing land now valuable and walled. The canal provided the means to move wool and slate for roofing to the mills of Lancashire, and as the looms began to clatter across the valleys of northern England, a new woodland based industry also began for Ambleside and the southern Lake District. The forestry skills of the local people, developed over the centuries in the production of charcoal, were exploited to coppice hundreds of acres of woodland. These were ideally placed to supply the demand for millions of bobbins for the mills. Harnessing the motive power of that commodity which in the Lake District is never scarce, water, bark and bobbin mills sprang up along every riverside, giving birth also to machine tool manufacture, mainly in the form of lathes to turn the wood for bobbins. A thriving trade in carrying and carting also developed and at last the area's road system evolved from muddy rutted tracks to reliable turnpike roads. Alongside Stock Beck, in Ambleside, as it rises towards the waterfalls in Stock Ghyll Park, are tall dark walls among the trees, in which you can see holes which used to support the axles of waterwheels. From North Road bridge, you look upon a replica of the wheel which once served the corn mill. Local bobbin manufacture declined towards the end of the 19th century, when cheaper sources were found elsewhere, but at the same time the gunpowder industry was growing, with the main local factory at Elterwater, supplying mines and quarries.

## Tourism and Wordsworth

The great textile mills of northern England produced new stratas of society. The mill owners, often from relatively humble but skilled origins, became enormously wealthy, the nouveau riche in fact. Ship owners too prospered as the colonies were exploited. At the same time, a new class of industrial workers developed, as poor country people migrated to the cities seeking employment. Both these new classes were to influence events in the area of Lake Windermere, which was still a remote and isolated part of England, and change its fortunes.

As conditions for all city dwellers deteriorated amid the smoke of the 'dark satanic mills', the wealthy northern industrialists used their fortunes to build grandiose summer mansions on the shores of Windermere. These lavish forerunners of today's more modest holiday home are dotted about for all to see. Many are now hotels or divided into apartments. The summer residences drew upon the local population for servants, gardeners and grooms, providing a new source of employment, the skills learnt there becoming of value in the slowly developing tourist trade.

The French revolution had seriously scared the British upper classes, whose tradition it was to undertake the 'Grand Tour' of European classical archaeological sites. This became impossible during the Napoleonic wars, but coincided with the birth of English Romanticism in literature, epitomised in the work of William Wordsworth and the Lake poets. Wordsworth was not the first to extol the natural beauty of the Lakeland landscape but his vision of it was enthusiastically embraced by the educated classes as a partial substitute for the Grand Tour and Ambleside became a popular destination for those seeking to immerse themselves in this new romantic movement.

As a result, by 1850 the area around Lake Windermere was gradually developing an increasingly important tourist trade, whose clients were wealthy and which although seasonal provided much needed income. Local entrepreneurs naturally wanted to expand this trade and the coming of the railway to Windermere gave them their chance. What had previously been the 'secret' preserve of the wealthy and the educated was now becoming accessible to the working man, desperate to escape, if only for a day on Bank Holidays, from the grime and pollution of the mill towns to the clean air of the countryside, which he had left only a generation or two before.

The demand for tourist facilities led to large scale development. The present Victorian houses and shops in Lake Road, Compston Road, Church Street and Rothay Road were built at this time. Sir George Gilbert Scott was commissioned to build a new Parish Church, St. Mary's.

## Exploitation and Preservation

Drawing upon the sentiment of the Romantics, a movement among the wealthy visitors and newly rich owners of local land was started to prevent further expansion of the railways and thus curb the opening up of the valleys 'to the vulgar gaze of the masses'. This led many years later to the formation of the National Trust, one of whose founders, Canon Rawnsley, lived in Grasmere at Allan Bank, the large private house which overlooks the lake from the north. Grasmere was in ancient times a more important parish than Ambleside, which had no church or consecrated burial ground.

Although the preservation movement won notable victories, including the prevention of a railway extension to Grasmere, it was destined to lose the war against mass tourism. It stopped the railways, but it could not stop buses and cars and as car ownership grew in the post-war years, tourism became a major industry, coinciding with the creation of National Parks which today manage the landscape and control development. The old industries, in woodlands, mines and quarries, declined and the demand for domestic servants dwindled away after the first world war. Farming became increasingly mechanised and less profitable, and diversification into alternative industry was severely proscribed by development restriction. Today tourism and its controlled building development has become the only major area of enterprise and employment, which is an increasingly vexatious issue, yet to be resolved.

From the earliest days of the conservation movement, local opinion was seldom sought or considered, the Lake District being perceived as a national asset for an educated elite rather than land from which its indigenous people needed to make a living. Thus began a conflict over the 'soul' of the Lake District, which has still not been resolved to many local people's satisfaction. Many resent the artificial halt to normal economic evolution imposed by the National Parks Acts.

# The Last 150 Years

Prosperity continued to grow, but due to its isolation, Ambleside was slow to develop modern standards of housing, public health and water supply. In 1855, the early feminist journalist Harriet Martineau (see Chapter 7) made her home at the Knoll, Ambleside, and undertook various surveys of the local population. She found poor standards of nutrition, sanitation and housing among a majority of what was then termed the peasantry. The condition of working people in Ambleside was dire. They were housed in hovels, often families of 12 or more inhabiting two squalid rooms. These conditions caused many working men to prefer the pub to their homes, resulting in what Harriet Martineau considered to be excessive drunkenness and poverty. (Nowadays of course there are decent homes for working people on pleasant estates. There just aren't enough of them and people cannot afford to buy them anyway.)

Modern developments in electricity and mains water followed in time, but the Langdale Valley did not get mains electricity until the 1960s. Even now, the area lags behind the nation in TV, radio and mobile phone reception

## Beggars Book for Ambleside

In the mid-nineteenth century Ambleside, like many other rural places, was a place where everyone knew each other and strangers were quickly spotted. There were not many visitors but there were people passing through, pedlars, tramps and itinerant workers. It was the job of the local constable to question such people, find out their business, assess their means and either move them on or if they had no money give them a 'ticket' which entitled them to stay for a night in the local tramps' lodging house. This is now the very comfortable Waterwheel Guest House in Bridge Street, otherwise known as Rattle Ghyll, or 'bug alley' by old locals in reference to the lack of hygiene of some of those then lodging there.

In the Armitt Library there are the original notebooks of one constable of the time, John Longmire.

Here are some extracts from 1848:

## March 9th, Thursday

Beggars gone at 8am. One tall strong man 6ft 3ins, a millwright and his woman. Saw them afterwards in the town singing. I ordered them away towards Keswick. They were clean and decently dressed. The man went back to the lodging house for his bundle.

## March 11th 1848

"Two men came to me for tickets – one a young man I ordered on to Grasmere. About 6 o'clock two other men, nail makers, saying they had no money, but I examined one of them and found a penny, and sixpence so I refused to give either of them tickets, they went away to the lodging house and paid for their beds and came back into the town to beg. I forbade them, they stayed about for more than an hour and were saucy. I gave them the choice whether they would go back to the lodging house or be put in the lock-up, they chose to go to the lodging house."

## March 11th 1848 (Saturday)

There was a silly daft young woman who had been in Mr. Jas. Green's out house all night so they sent for me. I took her 1d. cheese and 1d. bun for her to eat. Then I walked her up to beyond Low Wood Inn to be clear of her. Her name was Jane Wilson aged 26 years & from Lincolnshire.

The policy is plain – move them on, to Grasmere, Windermere, Keswick. So if you are caught misbehaving in Ambleside, beware! The aforementioned Felons Prosecutors could revive and banish you to one of those dreadful places!

Among Harriet Martineau's surveys was a Directory of the Lake District, a list of residents in 1855. The population has grown slightly since then to around 2500. The construction of the aqueduct from Thirlmere to Manchester in the 1880s brought an influx of Scottish workers, many of whom stayed on after the work was complete. Many Ambleside families joined the great emigration waves to the colonies and America, just as newcomers arrived to retire or to invest in tourism based businesses.

Here is a letter dated February 1832 from a London based agent, addressed to the "Overseers of the Parish of Ambleside":

Gentlemen,

We beg to acquaint you that we are ready to contract for the conveyance of Poor Persons or Paupers to the British Colonies in North America and the United States, and to Victual and find Bedding, if required by the Parish Authorities.

If London be too distant for embarkation, we will engage that a ship shall call at the nearest safe Port and there take them on board, provided a sufficient number of emigrants be offered..."

Old Ambleside and Grasmere family names listed by Miss Martineau include Airey, Atkinson, Backhouse, Bell, Benson, Birkett, Coward, Creighton, Dawson, Dixon, Dugdale, Elleray, Fisher, Garside, Hardisty, Hayes, Hodgson, Horrax, Jackson, Jenkinson, Lancaster, Mackereth, Martin, Newby, Newton, Nicholson, Robinson, Shepherd, Slee, Thompson, Tyson, Walker, Wilson, Woodburn, Woodend and

Woodhouse, almost all of whom have descendants still living in the district.

## Finally some statistics from the 2011 census:

In the 2011 census the population of Ambleside and Grasmere was 3,971 and was made up of approximately 50% females and 50% males. (Thank goodness for that!)

The average age of people in Ambleside and Grasmere is 46, while the median age is also 46.

88.0% of people living in Ambleside and Grasmere were born in England. 4% were born in other parts of Britain or Ireland.

95% of people living in Ambleside and Grasmere speak English. 3.5% speak an eastern European language.

The religious make up of Ambleside and Grasmere is 63.0% Christian, 24.4% No religion, 0.3% Muslim, 0.2% Jewish, 0.2% Atheist, 0.1% Buddhist, 0.1% Agnostic. (Not much chance of the National Park Authority being vexed by a planning application for a mosque or a synagogue then).

429 people did not state a religion. 20 people identified as a Jedi Knight. (Only 20??)

47.5% of people are married, 10.8% cohabit with a member of the opposite sex, 0.9% live with a partner of the same sex, 22.1% are single and have never married or been in a registered same sex partnership, 7.6% are separated or divorced. There are 187 widowed people living in Ambleside and Grasmere.

The top occupations listed by people in Ambleside and Grasmere are: Managers, directors and senior officials 21.8%, Skilled trades 16.9%, Other managers and proprietors 16.8%, Elementary 16.2%, Elementary administration and service 15.3%, Managers and Proprietors in Hospitality and Leisure Services 13.2%, Professional 9.1%, Sales and customer service 8.9%, Sales 8.5%, Associate professional and technical 7.8%.

# Epilogue

We hope this book has entertained and informed. If it hasn't, we failed but we can live with that. We hope you may have found parts of it amusing. If you didn't, it's best we don't meet.

If you already know Ambleside we hope you have found new things here. If you haven't been to Ambleside, we hope you will have been tempted to visit us. If the book has completely killed any desire you may have had to come here, you wouldn't have liked it anyway.

Constructive comment, corrections and suggestions for later editions are welcome at:
paul@ambleside.co.uk
or at
hello@sarahwaterhouse.org

# Index